EASY AND HEALTHY HOMEMADE DOG FOOD RECIPES AND GUIDE

IMPROVE DIGESTION, SOOTHE ALLERGIES, CONTROL WEIGHT, AND REDUCE DISEASE FOR ORAL HYGIENE, BRIGHTER COAT, AND ROBUST SKIN FOR A LONG, THRIVING LIFE

WHITLEY AUSTIN

PAGETURNER

This book is lovingly dedicated to my nine remarkable companions, each a unique soul that has filled my life with joy, laughter, and unconditional love. To Sky, whose boundless energy and bright spirit lift my days; Maggie May, whose gentle eyes and tender heart remind me of the purest form of love; Butter, the embodiment of warmth and comfort; and Shadow, my constant, faithful friend whose presence is my steady comfort.

To Mocha, with her rich, playful spirit that sweetens my life; Medianoche, the night's guardian whose loyalty knows no bounds; Kallie, whose grace and beauty illuminate the simplest moments; Gus, the embodiment of strength and loyalty, a steadfast protector; and Lakota, whose wise soul and serene presence bring peace to our lively home.

Each of you has taught me the essence of care, the value of patience, and the boundless possibilities of love. This book, a testament to our shared journey, is a tribute to your individuality, companionship, and the countless ways you enrich my life. May our days continue to be filled with shared adventures, quiet moments, and the creation of recipes that nourish both body and soul. Here's to many more meals prepared with love for my dearest Sky, Maggie May, Butter, Shadow, Mocha, Medianoche, Kallie, Gus, and Lakota.

In the eyes of every dog, we find the mirror to our soul, teaching us that love comes in the most wholesome and natural forms—like the meals we share, prepared with care and served with devotion.

— WHITLEY AUSTIN

CONTENTS

Introduction   xi

1. UNDERSTANDING THE BASICS OF CANINE
   NUTRITION   1
   The Essential Nutrients Your Dog Needs   1
   Understanding Your Dog's Dietary Needs   3
   Dangerous Foods to Avoid   5
   The Importance of Hydration: More Than Just a Drop
   in the Bucket   6

2. SWITCHING LANES: FROM STORE-BOUGHT TO
   HOMEMADE GOODNESS   11
   Gradual Transition: A Step-by-Step Guide   12
   Observing Your Dog's Reaction to the New Diet   13
   Dealing with a Picky Eater   15
   When to Consult a Vet During Transition   17

3. TAILORING MEALS TO YOUR DOG'S LIFE STAGE   21
   The Growing Puppy: Nutritional Needs and Feeding
   Schedule   21
   Turkey and Veggie Puppy Chow   22
   The Active Adult: Maintaining Optimum Health   24
   Beef and Veggie Power Bowl   24
   The Golden Years: Nutrition for Senior Dogs   27
   Chicken and Veggie Stew   28
   Dietary Adjustments for Pregnant and Nursing Dogs   30
   Lamb and Green Bean Feast   31

4. COMBATTING CANINE HEALTH CHALLENGES
   THROUGH NUTRITION   35
   Managing Allergies with a Specialized Diet   35
   Beef and Sweet Potato Dinner   36
   Duck and Pumpkin Stew   37
   Salmon and Peas Meal   38
   Recipes for Dogs with Digestive Issues   40
   Chicken and Pumpkin Puree   40
   Dietary Support for Dogs with Heart Disease   42

Turkey and Veggie Stir Fry   42

Salmon and Green Bean Medley   44

Nutritional Strategies for Weight Management   45

Chicken and Zucchini Stir Fry   46

One More Recipe for Weight Management   47

Turkey and Carrot Delight   47

5. FAST AND FLAVORFUL: QUICK HOMEMADE DOG
   FOOD RECIPES   51

Chicken and Vegetable Medley   52

Beef Stew for Dogs   54

Fish Delight: Salmon and Peas   56

Turkey and Brown Rice Dinner: A Nutrient-Rich Feast   58

6. FEEDING FIDO ON A BUDGET: COST-EFFECTIVE
   HOMEMADE RECIPES   63

Hearty Ground Turkey Mix   63

Chicken and Pumpkin Stew: A Bounty of Flavor on a
Budget   66

Beef and Quinoa Meal   68

Sweet Potato and Fish Feast   70

7. GRAIN-FREE GOODNESS: NOURISHING RECIPES
   FOR SENSITIVE TUMMIES   77

Chicken and Sweet Potato Grain-Free Dinner   77

Beef and Veggie Grain-Free Meal   80

Fish and Green Beans Grain-Free Recipe   82

Turkey and Carrots Grain-Free Feast   84

8. TANTALIZING TREATS AND SNACKS: SPOILING
   YOUR POOCH THE HEALTHY WAY   89

Peanut Butter and Banana Dog Biscuits: A Tail-
Wagging Delight   89

Chicken and Apple Doggie Treats: A Healthy
Indulgence   92

Sweet Potato Dog Chews: A Chewy Delight   94

Pumpkin and Oat Dog Cookies: A Crunchy Delight   96

9. MEAL PREPPING 101: MAKING HOMEMADE DOG
   FOOD EASIER   101

The Basics of Meal Prepping for Dogs   101

Safe Storage Practices for Homemade Dog Food:
Keeping it Fresh and Tasty   103

Preparing Large Batches: A Week's Worth of Meals 104

The Freeze-Thaw-Reheat Trio: Maximizing Meal
Longevity 106

10. THE RIGHT BITE: UNDERSTANDING AND
CALCULATING YOUR DOG'S PORTION SIZES 109

Determining Your Dog's Calorie Needs 109

Calculating Portion Sizes: It's All in the Details 111

Adjusting Portions for Weight Loss or Gain: The Scale
Balancing Act 113

Reading Your Dog's Hunger Signals: The Canine
Communication Code 115

11. SQUEEZING THE CLOCK: MAKING HOMEMADE
DOG FOOD IN A TIME CRUNCH 119

Overcoming Time Constraints: Every Minute Counts 119

Making Economically Smart Choices: Your Wallet's
Best Friend 122

Finding High-Quality Ingredients: The Treasure Hunt 124

Keeping Variety in Your Dog's Diet: The Spice of Life 126

12. PAW-SITIVE CHANGES: YOUR DOG'S HEALTH
TRANSFORMATION 131

Monitoring Health Changes after Switching to
Homemade Food 131

The Role of Regular Vet Checkups: Your Ally in
Canine Health 133

Celebrating Success Stories of Health Improvement 135

A Never-Ending Quest: Achieving Peak Canine
Health 137

Conclusion 143

A Word from the Author 146
References 149

FREE COLOR IMAGES AND FREE TRANSITION GUIDE

To Access FREE Full-Color Images of Recipes and Your FREE 31-Day Transition Guide, Scan the QR Code Below

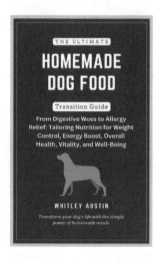

French Bulldogs are like charming little clowns with the heart of a philosopher; they spend half their time making you laugh and the other half pondering why they can't catch their tail.

INTRODUCTION

Well, hello there, fellow dog enthusiast! You're here because, like me, you believe our four legged friends are not just pets; they're family. And family deserves nothing but the best, right?

Let's talk about the joy of cooking for your best friend, the one with the wagging tail and the adorable, pleading eyes. The one who gives you unconditional love and thinks that you are, without a doubt, the most wonderful creature to grace this planet. You know who I mean.

Now, I'm not suggesting we whip up a Beef Wellington or a Coq au Vin for our pups, though I'm sure they wouldn't object. No, we're talking about simple, healthful, homemade dog food. It's about tailoring meals to our dogs' specific needs and tastes. It's about knowing exactly what goes into their bodies and having the peace of mind that comes with that knowledge.

In my own life, my wife Jackie and I have nine dogs - a lively and diverse bunch that keeps us on our toes and fills our hearts with joy. Their health and happiness are our top priorities, and that's why we're intrigued by the adventure of homemade dog food. We're not self-avowed experts. We're dog lovers just like you, and we desire to see firsthand the benefits of a homemade diet for dogs - the glossier coats, the increased energy, the overall zest for life. We hope our exploration is a total game-changer, to say the least.

The journey to healthier, happier dogs begins in your kitchen. It begins with fresh ingredients, a bit of time, and a whole lot of love. It begins with you. I'm excited to join you on this journey and to share with you the recipes that have captured our interest for our dogs.

Let's get cooking, shall we?

Labrador Retrievers are like the Google of dog breeds: they seem to know everything about fetching, swimming, and loving, but still think your every idea is fascinating!

1

UNDERSTANDING THE BASICS OF CANINE NUTRITION

D id you know that commercial dog food hasn't always been around? It's true! In fact, only about a hundred years ago, these products debuted on store shelves. Prior to that, dogs were eating what we were eating - real food made from scratch.

So, let's rewind the clock and get back to basics.

The Essential Nutrients Your Dog Needs

Proteins: The Building Blocks

Just like us, dogs need protein. It's an essential part of their diet and vital to every biological process. Think of proteins as the building blocks of your dog's body. They're used to build and repair tissues, make enzymes and hormones, and much more.

But where should this protein come from? Chicken, beef, and fish are all exceptional sources. These are 'complete proteins' because they contain all your dog's required amino acids.

Now, let's say you're preparing a meal and have some chicken at hand. You might be tempted to toss a few pieces into the pot, bones and all. But hold on a minute! Cooking bones changes their structure, making them more likely to splinter and cause serious harm to your dog. So, always make sure to remove any bones before cooking.

Carbohydrates: Energy Providers

Next up are carbohydrates. They give your dog energy, help maintain a healthy gut, and keep their brains ticking over. Sweet potatoes and brown rice are fantastic sources of carbs for your dog.

Why sweet potatoes, you ask? They're fortified in dietary fiber, which aids digestion, and they're also packed with vitamins and minerals. As for brown rice, it's a whole grain, meaning it's much more nutritious than its white counterpart. It's also gentle on the stomach, making it a good option for dogs with sensitive tummies.

Fats: Not the Enemy

Fats often get a bad rap, but they're essential for your dog's health. They provide energy, support cell function, and help keep your dog's skin and coat healthy.

Good sources of fats for your dog include fish oil and flaxseed. Fish oil is replete with omega-3 fatty acids, which have anti-inflammatory characteristics and contribute to a shiny, healthy coat. Flaxseed, on the other hand, is a plant-based source of omega-3, making it an excellent option for dogs on a plant-based diet.

Vitamins and Minerals: Small but Mighty

Last but certainly not least are vitamins and minerals. These tiny nutrients pack a punch for your dog's health. They're involved in everything from bone health to immune function to nerve conduction.

Fresh fruits and vegetables are nature's multivitamins. They're packed with vitamins and minerals to help keep your dog in tip-top shape. For example, carrots are rich in beta-carotene, converted into vitamin A in your dog's body. Vitamin A is essential for vision, growth, and immune function.

Similarly, apples are high in vitamin C, which is necessary for collagen synthesis and has antioxidant properties. Just make sure to remove the seeds before feeding apples to your dog because they carry a component that can be toxic in large quantities.

So there you have it - the four main nutrient groups that your dog needs: proteins, carbohydrates, fats, and vitamins and minerals. Remember, the key is balance. Just like you wouldn't eat only chicken or sweet potatoes, your dog needs various nutrients to stay healthy. By providing a wide range of whole foods, you're setting your dog up for a long, happy life by your side.

Sure, it might not be as easy as just opening a can of dog food, but the peace of mind that comes with knowing what your dog is eating is worth the extra effort. Plus, it's pretty darn satisfying to see your dog's tail wagging like crazy as you set down a bowl of homemade goodness. So grab your apron, pull out that cutting board, and let's get cooking!

Understanding Your Dog's Dietary Needs

Puppy Nutrient Requirements

Let's kick things off with the little ones - our puppies. If you've ever had a puppy, you know they're balls of energy. One minute, they zoom around the house, and the next, they're passed out on the floor.

Puppies need a diet high in protein to fuel all that playing and growing. We're talking about 22-28% of their diet. Why so high? Think about it this way. You're building a house, and protein is your bricks. It would be best if you had as many of them as possible to complete the job.

But that's not all. Puppies need more fat than adult dogs, as well. About 8-10% of their diet should be fat. This helps sustain their energy levels and support brain development.

Lastly, puppies need a good amount of calcium and phosphorus for their growing bones. For every 1,000 calories, they need about 3 grams of calcium and 2.5 grams of phosphorus. It's like the cement that holds the bricks together.

Adult Dog Nutrient Requirements

Next up, we have our adult dogs. Now that they're fully grown, their nutritional needs change. They aren't growing anymore, so they need less protein - about 18-25% of their diet.

Fat should comprise 5-8% of an adult dog's diet. While they don't need as much as puppies, fat is essential for maintaining healthy skin and a shiny coat.

As for vitamins and minerals, adult dogs need a balanced diet to ensure they're getting all the necessary nutrients. This is where a variety of fruits and vegetables come in. They're packed with vitamins and minerals, adding nice texture and flavor to your dog's meals.

Senior Dog Nutrient Requirements

Last but certainly not least, we have our senior dogs. As dogs age, their metabolism slows down, and they become less active. This means they need fewer calories to avoid weight gain.

Protein should make up about 20% of a senior dog's diet. Despite what some people believe, old dogs should not be on a low-protein diet. Protein is crucial for maintaining muscle mass, which declines with age.

Fat should make up about 5% of a senior dog's diet. While they need less than younger dogs, fat is still crucial for keeping their skin and coat healthy.

Finally, senior dogs need a balanced diet to get all the necessary vitamins and minerals. Some old dogs may have difficulty absorbing certain nutrients, so providing a variety of nutrient-dense foods is crucial.

Remember, every dog is unique, and these are just general guidelines. Your dog's breed, size, activity level, and health status affect their nutritional needs. When in doubt, consult with your vet. They can provide personalized advice based on your dog's specific needs.

So that's the basic rundown, the nutritional needs of puppies, adult dogs, and seniors. With this knowledge, you're one step closer to whipping up balanced, nutritious meals for your dog. But before we dive into the recipes, let's take a moment to talk about some foods that might seem harmless but can actually be dangerous for dogs.

Dangerous Foods to Avoid

Chocolate and Coffee: A Bitter Truth

Now, I know what you're thinking. "What? Chocolate and coffee? But I love those!" Trust me, I feel your pain. But when it comes to our furry friends, these treats are a big no-no. They contain substances called theobromine and caffeine, which are toxic to dogs. Ingestion can lead to restlessness, rapid breathing, muscle tremors, and, in severe cases, seizures. So, next time you're sipping your morning coffee or indulging in a chocolate bar, remember to keep it out of your dog's reach.

Grapes and Raisins: Small but Deadly

Next on the list are grapes and raisins. Yes, those sweet, bite-sized fruits that are so easy to pop into your mouth. Unfortunately, they're toxic to dogs. Scientists aren't entirely sure why, but even a tiny amount can cause kidney failure in dogs. So, keep that bowl of grapes on the high counter, and make sure your dog doesn't have access to your morning bowl of raisin bran.

Onions and Garlic: Hidden Dangers

Onions and garlic might be staples in your kitchen, but they harm dogs. They contain compounds that can damage your dog's red blood cells, leading to hemolytic anemia. Symptoms include weakness, pale gums, and breathlessness. Moreover, the toxic effects are cumulative and can build up over time. So, even small amounts ingested regularly can be harmful. When cooking for your dog, leave these ingredients out of the pot.

Avocado and Macadamia Nuts: Not All Healthy Foods Are Dog-Friendly

Finally, we have avocado and macadamia nuts. Now, I know what you're thinking, "But aren't those healthy?" Yes, for humans, but not for our pups. Avocados contain persin, which can upset your dog's stomach. And while macadamia nuts might be a healthy snack for you, they can cause weakness, vomiting, tremors, and hyperthermia in dogs.

Navigating the world of dog nutrition can feel like walking through a minefield. But don't worry; it becomes second nature with some knowledge and practice. Remember, when in doubt, always err on the side of caution. And if you suspect your dog has eaten something they shouldn't have, contact your vet immediately.

So, we've covered the nutrients your dog needs and the foods they should avoid. But there's another critical piece of the puzzle we haven't touched on yet - hydration. Many people overlook the importance of water in their dog's diet, but it's just as essential as any nutrient. Let's examine why hydration matters and how you can ensure your dog gets enough.

The Importance of Hydration: More Than Just a Drop in the Bucket

Hydration is something we rarely give a second thought to. We get thirsty, we drink. Simple, right? But for our dogs, hydration is more complex. As their caregivers, it's our responsibility to ensure they're getting enough water.

Think about this: while food provides some moisture, a dog's primary source of hydration is the water we provide. Water plays a vital role in your dog's health, from aiding digestion to maintaining body temperature to transporting nutrients in the blood. Our dogs can quickly become dehydrated without adequate water intake, leading to serious health issues.

Signs of Dehydration: When to Sound the Alarm

How can you tell if your dog is dehydrated? It's not like they can tell you they're feeling parched. But there are signs you can look out for.

A dehydrated dog might seem less active or lazy. Your dog's eyes could appear sunken, and their gums might feel dry or sticky. If you gently pinch their skin, it may not spring back as quickly as usual.

These are all warning signs that your dog could be dehydrated and need immediate attention. But remember, prevention is always better than cure.

Providing Fresh Water: It's a Round-the-Clock Job

The first step in preventing hydration is ensuring your dog always has access to fresh water. Whether at home, out for a walk, or on a road trip, ensure there's always a water source available for your dog.

And no, that doesn't mean leaving out a bowl of water in the morning and calling it a day. Water can quickly become contaminated with dust, debris, or even bugs. So, ensure you're refreshing your dog's water multiple times daily.

Hydrating Foods: Sneaking in Extra Sips

You can boost your dog's hydration through their diet in addition to providing fresh water. Various fruits and vegetables are high in water content and can be a good source of extra hydration.

Take watermelon, for example. It's made up of 92% water and is a tasty, hydrating treat for your dog on a hot summer day. Remove the seeds, and do not give your dog the rind.

Cucumbers are another hydrating food you can add to your dog's diet. With a water content of 95%, they're a super refreshing snack. Plus, they're low in calories and high in nutrients, making them a fantastic choice for dogs on a diet.

But let's remember our main meals. If you're preparing homemade food for your dog, add some low-sodium broth or water to their meals for a hydration boost. Not only will it add moisture, but it'll also make their meals even more delicious.

Hydration for your dog is a simple part of their care, but it's crucial.

As we wrap up this chapter, let's take a moment to reflect on what we've covered. We've talked about the essential nutrients your dog needs, how to meet their dietary needs at different life stages, foods to avoid, and the importance of hydration.

It's a lot to take in, but don't worry, you've got this! You're already showing your commitment to your dog's health by being here and reading this, and that's half the battle won.

So, pat yourself on the back, give your dog a scratch behind the ears, and let's get ready to put all this knowledge into action. Up next? We're going to tackle the topic of tailoring meals to your dog's life stage. Prepare to get personal with your pup's plate! Let's do this together!

German Shepherds are the multitasking wizards of the dog world; they can go from zero to hero in the blink of an eye, guarding the house with vigilance one minute and offering cuddles the next, all while maintaining that 'I'm on top of everything' hairdo.

2

SWITCHING LANES: FROM STORE-BOUGHT TO HOMEMADE GOODNESS

Remember the first time you tried riding a bike? You started with training wheels, gradually getting the feel of the bike beneath you. And one day, you took off those training wheels, wobbling a bit before gaining balance and pedaling away. Transitioning your dog from store-bought to homemade food is quite similar. It requires patience, attention, and a smooth, gradual transition. A sudden switch can upset your dog's stomach, leading to digestive issues. But fear not, fellow dog devotees! I'm here to guide you through this transition, ensuring a smooth and successful shift towards homemade goodness.

Making homemade dog food can seem daunting, especially if you're accustomed to the convenience of store-bought food. But the benefits - knowing precisely what's in your dog's bowl, tailoring recipes to their specific needs, and providing them with fresh, wholesome meals - are well worth the effort. So, please put on your apron, grab your ingredients, and let's embark on this exciting culinary venture!

Gradual Transition: A Step-by-Step Guide

Mixing Homemade with Store-Bought: The Initial Phase

Think of this as the training wheels phase. You start by mixing a small amount of homemade food with your dog's usual store-bought food. This allows your dog to get used to the new flavors and textures without drastically changing their diet.

For example, if your dog usually eats a cup of store-bought food, you might start by replacing a quarter with homemade food. This means you'll serve a three-quarters cup of store-bought food and a quarter cup of homemade food.

Slowly Increasing Homemade Ratio: Gaining Balance

Once your dog is comfortable with this new mix, it's time to gradually increase the amount of homemade food. You might go from a quarter to a half, then from a half to three-quarters, until you're serving entirely homemade meals.

Imagine you're driving on a highway and need to switch lanes. You don't just swerve into the next lane. You switch on your indicator, check your mirrors, and gradually move over. The same principle applies here. The change should be slow and steady, giving your dog's digestive system time to adjust.

Monitoring for Digestive Upsets: Keep an Eye Out

Transitioning to a new diet can sometimes lead to digestive upsets. You might notice changes in your dog's stool or increased gas. These are usually temporary and should resolve as your dog adjusts to their new diet. But it's necessary to monitor your dog closely during this transition period.

Think of yourself as a detective, looking for any changes or clues that something might be amiss. If you notice persistent diarrhea, vomiting, or any other concerning symptoms, it's best to consult your vet. They can help you determine whether these symptoms are a normal part of the transition or if they indicate an underlying issue.

Baking a cake is an art. You can't rush the process by cranking up the oven temperature. It takes patience and precise measurements to create a delectable dessert. The same goes for transitioning your dog to homemade food. It's a gradual process that requires patience, attention, and a keen eye for potential hiccups.

Therefore, seize your measuring cup, pull up your sleeves, and prepare to whip up some homemade delights for your four-legged companion. Remember, this transition is not just about changing your dog's diet. It's about enhancing their health, extending their lifespan, and enriching their lives with fresh, wholesome meals made with love. And there's no better chef for the job than you!

Observing Your Dog's Reaction to the New Diet

Energy Levels: The Pep in Their Step

As you begin to replace store-bought food with homemade meals, one of the first changes you might notice is in your dog's energy levels. Food is fuel for our bodies, and the quality of that fuel can significantly impact how we feel and function. It's the same for our canine companions.

Switching to homemade food may give your dog a natural energy boost. This isn't about your furry friend bouncing off the walls (although puppies might do that anyway). Still, instead, it's about them having a consistent energy level to enjoy their daily walks, play sessions, and even those spontaneous zoomies around the living room.

Watch for changes in energy levels during different parts of the day. Are they more eager for their morning walk? Do they still have energy for a game of fetch in the afternoon? Noting these changes can help you gauge how well your dog adjusts to their new diet.

Coat Condition: Shine On, You Crazy Diamond

Your dog's coat can reveal a lot about their overall health. A shiny, smooth coat is often a sign of good nutrition, while a dull, dry, or brittle coat might indicate a nutritional deficiency.

One of the many benefits of homemade dog food is it can improve your dog's coat condition. Fresh, whole foods are rich in essential fatty acids like Omega-3 and Omega-6, key players in maintaining skin and coat health. These fatty acids help sustain your dog's skin from the inside out, leading to a softer, shinier coat.

Does their fur feel softer or look shinier? Are there fewer flakes when you scratch their belly? These can be signs that the new diet is benefiting your dog.

Stool Consistency: Yes, We're Going There

Let's talk about poop. It may not be the most glamorous of topics, but when it comes to your dog's health, it's an important one. The size, shape, and consistency of your dog's stool can provide valuable clues about their digestive health and how well they're adjusting to their new diet.

Switching to homemade dog food can change your dog's stool. The increased fiber content in fresh, whole foods can result in larger, firmer stools. On the other hand, if your dog's system is having trouble adjusting, they might experience loose stools or diarrhea.

Take note of any changes in your dog's stool consistency. Are the stools firmer or softer than usual? Are they larger or smaller? Are they a different color? If you notice any drastic changes or your dog seems to be straining or uncomfortable, it might be time to consult your vet.

Navigating these diet changes can feel like playing detective. You're watching for clues, noting changes, and piecing together the puzzle of your dog's nutritional health. It's an integral part of the process and can bring you closer to your four-legged friend. After all, who else but the most devoted of dog lovers would find themselves assessing the shininess of their dog's coat or the consistency of their poop? It's all part of the journey and a testament to the incredible lengths we go to for our pets. Because they're not just dogs, they're family. And there's no mountain too high, no valley too low, and yes, no poop too stinky for us when it comes to their well-being. So, as you continue on this path, remember that every observation, every small victory, and every hurdle is a step towards a happier, healthier life for your dog.

Dealing with a Picky Eater

You've done your research, gathered your ingredients, and lovingly prepared a homemade meal for your four-legged friend. You set the bowl down, expecting your dog to dive right in, but instead, they sniff it, give you a look, and walk away. If this sounds familiar, welcome to the club of pet parents with picky eaters!

Introducing New Foods Slowly: Patience Is Key

Imagine being served a dish you've never seen or tasted before. You may be hesitant to try it. The same goes for our dogs. A sudden change in their diet can be a shock to their system. This is why it's essential to introduce new foods slowly.

Start by adding a small amount of the new food to their usual meal. This allows your dog to get used to the unique flavors and textures gradually. Over time, you can slowly increase the amount of new food while decreasing the amount of their old food.

Think of it like getting into a swimming pool. You don't just jump right in. You start by dipping your toes, then your feet, and gradually, you immerse yourself completely. Slowly introducing new foods makes the experience more comfortable for your dog and increases the chances of them accepting the fresh food.

Using Tasty Toppers: The Icing on the Cake

We all love a little extra something on our food, whether a dollop of whipped cream on our hot chocolate or a sprinkle of cheese on our pasta. The same can be true for our dogs. Adding a tasty topper to your dog's meal can make it more appealing and entice your picky eater to dig in.

Tasty toppers can be anything from a spoonful of low-sodium chicken broth to a sprinkle of shredded cheese. You could even use a bit of their favorite wet dog food. Remember, the goal is not to drown their meal in toppers but to enhance the flavor and make it more enticing.

It's like adding a cherry on top of a cake. The cherry doesn't change the cake itself; it adds a touch of color and makes the cake look more appetizing. Similarly, using tasty toppers can pique your dog's interest and make their mealtime more enjoyable.

Positive Reinforcement: Celebrate the Small Wins

Remember how good it felt when you were praised for doing something right? Our dogs feel the same way. Positive reinforcement can help encourage your picky eater to try new foods.

When your dog takes a bite of their new food, give them lots of praise and affection. This helps them associate trying new foods with positive experiences. Over time, this can make them more willing to try new foods.

Think of it as cheering on a runner in a race. Your encouragement can give them the boost they need to continue and cross the finish line. Similarly, your praise and affection can motivate your picky eater to try their new food and, eventually, finish their meal.

Guiding a picky eater is a challenge. Still, you can help your dog embrace their new homemade diet with patience, creativity, and lots of love. Remember, this isn't just about feeding them. It's about nourishing them with wholesome, homemade food that supports their health and well-being. And no one better equipped for this task than you, their loving and devoted pet parent. So, hold on to your chef's hat, my friend. This culinary adventure is only just beginning!

When to Consult a Vet During Transition

Visualize learning a new dance routine. You have the steps down, but now and then, you stumble. That's okay because your dance instructor is there to guide you, correct your movements, and help you perfect your performance. Similarly, your vet is your go-to guide as you transition your dog to homemade food. They're there to offer advice, address concerns, and assist you in ensuring your dog's health and well-being throughout this transition.

Persistent Digestive Upsets: When the Going Gets Tough

Let's start with the topic no one likes to discuss - digestive upsets. While a certain degree of digestive upset can be expected during the transition to homemade food, persistent or severe symptoms cause concern.

Think of it like this - you're on a boat, and the water is choppy. A little bit of seasickness is to be expected. But if the sea sickness persists even after you're back on solid ground, it's time to seek medical help.

Suppose your dog experiences ongoing diarrhea, vomiting, or constipation despite a gradual transition and careful introduction of new foods. In that case, it's time to consult your vet. These symptoms can indicate your dog is having difficulty adjusting to the new diet, or an underlying health issue must be addressed.

Weight Loss or Gain: The Scale Doesn't Lie

Next up, let's talk about weight changes. Like us, our dogs can gain or lose weight based on their diet, exercise, and overall health.

During the transition to homemade food, monitoring your dog's weight is essential. If you see significant weight loss or gain, it's time to pick up the phone and call your vet.

Weight loss can indicate your dog needs more calories or nutrients from their new diet. On the other hand, weight gain can mean that they're getting too many calories. Both scenarios can have long-term effects on your dog's health, so it's crucial to address these changes immediately.

Changes in Behavior or Energy Levels: Reading Between the Lines

Lastly, let's take a moment to talk about changes in behavior or energy levels. Our dogs can't tell us in words when they're not feeling well, but they can show us through their actions.

If you notice your dog is less active than usual, reluctant to play, or showing signs of discomfort or distress, it's time to consult your vet. Similarly, if your dog seems overly hyper or restless, this could also be a sign that something's amiss.

Behavior or energy level changes can indicate your dog is not responding well to their new diet. It could be an ingredient that does not agree with them, a lack of certain nutrients, or an excess of others. It's like trying a new workout routine. Suppose you suddenly start feeling lethargic or experiencing muscle pain. In that case, you should consult a health professional to determine what's going wrong.

In all these scenarios, your vet is your most reliable resource. They can help you identify the cause of these changes and guide you on the right path toward a successful transition to homemade food.

Switching to homemade dog food is a commitment to your dog's health and happiness. It's about taking charge of your dog's nutrition and providing the best quality food you can offer. Yes, it might seem daunting, but it's an entirely achievable goal with the proper guidance, patience, and a pinch of love.

So, don't be discouraged if you hit a few bumps. Remember, you're not alone on this path. Your vet is there to help. I'm here to provide practical knowledge and delicious recipes to make this transition easier.

Remember, every step you take on this adventure is a step forward to your beloved dog's healthier, happier, and longer life. You're not just their owner; you're their hero. And that, my friend, is the most rewarding part of this whole adventure.

So, let's keep going. We have more recipes to explore, tips to share, and ways to enrich your dog's life through homemade food. Onwards to the next chapter, we'll dive into quick and easy dog meals that are as delicious as they are nutritious.

Poodles: the brainiacs of the dog park, sporting more hairstyles than a pop star and the intelligence to know they're pulling every look off. They're like the sophisticated scholars of the canine world; only their dissertations are on the optimal techniques for fetching tennis balls and mastering the art of the dignified snoot.

3

TAILORING MEALS TO YOUR DOG'S LIFE STAGE

L et's picture this: You and your adorable, wiggly bundle of joy - your puppy - are at the park. You're playing fetch and amazed at the boundless energy this little creature possesses. Like human babies, puppies are in a stage of rapid growth and development. They're building their muscles, strengthening their bones, and learning new daily skills. And to fuel all this activity and growth, they need a special diet.

The Growing Puppy: Nutritional Needs and Feeding Schedule

High Protein Recipes: Your Puppy's Building Blocks

Your puppy's diet should be a high-energy, high-protein one. Think of protein as the building blocks for your puppy's growing body. It promotes healthy growth and development and supports their immune system.

Here's a simple, high-protein recipe for your puppy:

Turkey and Veggie Puppy Chow

Serving Size:

- For smaller meals (1/4 cup), this recipe would yield approximately 16 to 24 servings.
- For larger meals (1/2 cup), it would yield approximately 8 to 12 servings.

Ingredients:

- 1 pound ground turkey
- 2 cups of cooked brown rice
- 1 cup of carrots, chopped
- 1 cup of peas
- 1 tablespoon of fish oil (optional)

Instructions:

1. Cook the ground turkey in a non-stick pan over medium heat until it's well-cooked.
2. Combine the cooked turkey, brown rice, carrots, and peas in a large pot.
3. Cook the mixture over medium heat for about 15 minutes or until the vegetables are soft.
4. Let it cool before serving. If you're using fish oil, you can stir it in now.

This recipe is packed with protein from the turkey, and the brown rice provides the carbohydrates your puppy needs for energy. The carrots and peas offer a great source of vitamins and minerals. At the same time, the optional fish oil can increase their intake of omega-3 fatty acids for a shiny, healthy coat.

Feeding Frequency: Little and Often

When feeding your puppy, the key is to offer small meals frequently. Puppies have small stomachs but significant energy needs, so they need to eat more often than adult dogs.

Most puppies should be fed three to four times a day. Depending on your puppy's age, size, and breed, this can be adjusted. Larger breeds may require more frequent feedings, while smaller breeds may do well with three meals a day.

Remember, every puppy is unique, and their feeding schedule can also depend on their metabolism and activity. So, discussing your puppy's feeding schedule with your vet is always a good idea.

Portion Sizes: Not Too Little, Not Too Much

Getting the portion sizes right is a crucial part of feeding your puppy. If you give your puppy too little food, they may not get the nutrients they need for healthy growth. Too much food and your puppy can become overweight, leading to many health problems.

But how do you figure out how much to feed your puppy?

Following the dog food package's feeding guidelines is a good rule of thumb. These are usually based on your puppy's weight. As an example, if your puppy weighs 10 pounds, and the feeding guide recommends 1 cup of food for every 10 pounds of body weight, you would feed your puppy 1 cup of food per meal.

However, these guidelines are just that - guidelines. Every puppy is different, and their feeding needs can vary. Their breed, size, activity level, and metabolism affect how much food they need.

So, keep a close eye on your puppy. If they look plump, you should cut back on their portions. If they're looking thin, they might need more food. And if you need more clarification, always consult with your vet. The vet can provide personalized advice based on your puppy's specific needs.

Puppy Feeding Checklist

Here's a quick checklist to help you manage your puppy's feeding:

- High-protein meals? Check.
- Regular, small meals? Check.
- Correct portion sizes? Check.
- Normal weight and health checks? Check.
- Personalized advice from your vet? Check.

With all this information, you're ready to meet your growing puppy's nutritional needs head-on. Roll up your sleeves, arm yourself with your spoon, and get ready to whip up some delicious, high-protein meals for your little one. Your puppy's future health and happiness start in your kitchen, and there's no better chef for the job than you!

The Active Adult: Maintaining Optimum Health

Balanced Diet Recipes: A Symphony of Nutrients

Now, we're sailing into the prime of your dog's life - adulthood. The chaotic puppy days are behind you, and you're currently looking at a fully grown, active adult dog. Like humans, adult dogs need a well-rounded diet to keep them in tip-top shape.

Imagine a symphony orchestra. Each instrument plays a different part, but together, the instruments create a beautiful piece of music. Similarly, your adult dog's diet should be a symphony of nutrients, each playing its own part in contributing to their overall health.

Let's whip up a balanced, nutritious recipe for your adult dog:

Beef and Veggie Power Bowl

Serving Size:

- For small breeds (½ to 1 cup per meal), the recipe could provide around 7 to 14 servings.
- For medium breeds (1 to 2.5 cups per meal), it would yield approximately 3 to 7 servings.
- For large breeds (2.5 to 4 cups per meal), it might yield about 2 to 3 servings.

Ingredients:

- 2 pounds lean ground beef
- 2 cups cooked quinoa
- 1 cup carrots, diced
- 1 cup peas
- 1 cup green beans, chopped
- 1 tablespoon olive oil (optional)

Instructions:

1. Brown the ground beef in a non-stick pan over medium heat until fully cooked.
2. Mix the cooked beef, quinoa, carrots, peas, and green beans in a large pot.
3. Simmer the mixture over medium heat for 15 minutes or until the veggies are tender.
4. Let it cool before serving. If you're using olive oil, you can mix it in now.

This recipe is packed with protein from beef and quinoa, a complete protein that provides a good fiber dose. The veggies add a burst of vitamins and minerals; the optional olive oil is an excellent source of healthy fats.

Monitoring Weight: Keeping the Scales Balanced

As your dog grows into adulthood, keeping an eye on their weight is crucial. Overweight dogs, just like overweight humans, can face numerous health issues, from joint problems to heart disease. Conversely, underweight dogs may not get the nutrients they need to stay healthy.

But how do you know if your dog is at a healthy weight? Aside from regular vet check-ups, there are a few things you can look out for.

When you look at your dog from the side, you should be able to see a nice tuck at their waist. And when you look at them from above, you should see a clear waistline. If your dog is more sausage-shaped, they might carry a few extra pounds.

You should also be able to feel your dog's ribs easily when you run your hands along their sides. If you must press hard to feel them, your dog might be overweight. If the ribs are very prominent, your dog might be underweight.

If you're worried about your dog's weight, don't hesitate to contact your vet. Your regular vet can provide personalized advice based on your dog's breed, size, age, and overall health.

Regular Exercise: Playtime with a Purpose

We all know exercise is essential for our health; the same goes for our dogs. Regular physical activity helps to keep your dog's weight in check, strengthens their muscles, keeps their joints flexible, and can even help prevent behavioral problems.

The quantity of exercise your dog needs can depend on their breed, age, and health. Typically, dogs require a minimum of one hour of daily exercise, although certain energetic breeds might need additional activity.

Walking is an excellent form of exercise for dogs and humans alike. It provides physical exercise and allows your dog to explore their environment, which can provide mental stimulation.

Playtime can also be a great form of exercise. Games like fetch, tug-of-war, or hide-and-seek can keep your dog active and engaged.

Remember that each dog is an individual, and a strategy effective for one may not suit another. The most important thing is to find activities that you both enjoy. This not only ensures that your dog gets the exercise they need, but it also strengthens the bond between you.

So, here are a few keys to maintaining your adult dog's health. With balanced nutrition, regular weight checks, and plenty of exercise, you're well on your way to ensuring your dog enjoys their adult years in the best health possible. So let's keep the ball rolling - or, shall we say, the tail wagging!

The Golden Years: Nutrition for Senior Dogs

Ah, the golden years! The playful puppy days are fond memories, and the active adult years have mellowed into a slower, more relaxed pace. Your dog, your faithful companion, has been with you through thick and thin, and now, they're stepping into their senior years. As your dog ages, their nutritional needs change, and it's up to you to navigate these changes and provide them with the best care possible. Let's get started, shall we?

Low Fat Recipes: Light on Fat, Heavy on Love

As dogs age, their metabolism decreases, leading to reduced activity levels. This means they need fewer calories to avoid gaining weight. One way to reduce calorie intake is by offering low-fat meals. But remember, low fat doesn't have to mean low flavor. With the right ingredients, you can whip up delicious, low-fat meals that your senior dog will love.

Here's a simple, low-fat recipe for your senior dog:

Chicken and Veggie Stew

Serving Size:

- For small breeds (½ to ¾ cup per meal), the recipe could provide around 9 to 18 servings.
- For medium breeds (¾ to 1½ cups per meal), it would yield approximately 5 to 9 servings.
- For large breeds (1½ to 2½ cups per meal), it might yield about 3 to 5 servings.

Ingredients:

- 2 pounds of skinless chicken breast
- 2 cups cooked brown rice
- 1 cup carrots, diced
- 1 cup green beans, chopped
- 1 tablespoon olive oil (optional)

Instructions:

1. In a non-stick pan, cook the chicken breast over medium heat until it's fully cooked.
2. Mix the cooked chicken, brown rice, carrots, and green beans in a large pot.
3. Simmer the mixture over medium heat for 15 minutes or until the veggies are tender.
4. Let it cool before serving. If you're using olive oil, you can mix it in now.

This recipe is low in fat but packed with lean protein from the chicken. The brown rice offers a beneficial fiber content. At the same time, the vegetables contribute a burst of color and enhance the dish with essential vitamins and minerals.

Joint Health Supplements: Supporting the Springs in Their Step

As dogs get older, their joints can start to wear out, leading to conditions like arthritis. While a balanced diet is essential, sometimes, your dog might need extra help. This is where joint health supplements come in.

Several supplements on the market can support your dog's joint health. Glucosamine and chondroitin are popular choices. They help maintain the health of your dog's cartilage, the flexible tissue cushions their joints.

Fish oil supplements, commonly rich in Omega-3 fatty acids, can also benefit joint health. These substances possess anti-inflammatory qualities and can aid in alleviating joint pain and stiffness.

Before starting any supplement regimen, talking to your vet is essential. He can recommend the right supplements and dosages for your dog's needs.

Regular Vet Check-ups: A Stitch in Time Saves Nine

Regular vet check-ups are vital at every stage of your dog's life, but they become even more important as your dog ages. Elderly dogs are at a greater risk of health problems, and detecting these issues at a younger age can significantly impact their treatment and management.

Your dog will be thoroughly examined from head to tail at a veterinary check-up. The vet will assess their weight, monitor the heart and lungs, inspect the eyes and ears, and evaluate the health of their teeth and gums. They'll also ask about your dog's diet, exercise, and general behavior.

These check-ups are also an excellent opportunity to ask questions or discuss your concerns. Remember, you know your dog best. If you notice any changes in their behavior, appetite, or physical condition, don't hesitate to bring it up.

Senior dogs hold a special place in our hearts. They've been our loyal companions for years, and as they step into their golden years, they deserve nothing but the best. With the proper diet, extra joint support, and regular vet check-ups, you can ensure your senior dog enjoys the golden years in good health and happiness.

So, go ahead. Whip up that low-fat chicken stew, add that joint supplement to their meal, and schedule that vet check-up. Your senior dog might not be able to thank you in words, but their wagging tail and contented sighs as they settle in for a nap will say it all. After all, love isn't just petting and playtime. It's also about providing the care they need, from puppyhood to the golden years.

Now, let's move on to a particular group of dogs requiring extra care regarding nutrition - pregnant and nursing dogs. Just like human moms-to-be, pregnant and nursing dogs have unique nutritional needs. So, put on your chef's hat, and let's dive into the world of nutrition for pregnant and nursing dogs.

Dietary Adjustments for Pregnant and Nursing Dogs

Allow me to paint a picture for you. Your beloved furry companion is soon to be a proud parent. You're preparing for the patter of tiny paws and looking forward to the joy and chaos that puppies bring. Your dog is pregnant, and just like human mothers-to-be, her body is transforming significantly. And these changes aren't just physical. Her dietary needs are changing, too.

Increased Caloric Intake: Fueling Two Lives

Our first pit-stop on this culinary adventure is the world of calories. Now, don't groan. I know the word 'calories' often brings to mind diets and restrictions, but in the world of pregnant dogs, it's all about abundance. You see, your pregnant dog isn't just eating for one anymore. Her body is fueling the growth and development of her puppies, too. This means she needs more calories than usual.

It's like packing for a long trip. You wouldn't just throw a few items into your suitcase and hope for the best. No, you make a list, pack enough for your journey, and then add a few extra items, just in case. Similarly, when feeding your pregnant dog, you must ensure you supply enough calories for her journey through pregnancy and then some.

But remember, the goal isn't to overfeed your dog. It's about providing the necessary calories without contributing to unnecessary weight gain. So, how do you achieve this? The answer lies in offering nutrient-dense foods and adjusting portion sizes per your vet's advice.

Extra Protein Recipes: Building Blocks for Puppies

Our next station on this culinary tour is protein land. Protein is the building material if calories are the fuel for your pregnant dog's journey. It's vital for the growth and development of her puppies. But how do you ensure your pregnant dog is getting enough protein? By offering her protein-rich meals, of course!

Here's a simple, protein-packed recipe you can try:

Lamb and Green Bean Feast

Serving Size:

- For smaller meals (1/4 cup), this recipe would yield approximately 28 to 36 servings
- For larger meals (1/2 cup), it would yield around 14 to 18 servings

Ingredients:

- 2 pounds of ground lamb
- 2 cups cooked quinoa
- 1 cup carrots, chopped
- 1 cup green beans, chopped
- 1 tablespoon olive oil (optional)

Instructions:

1. Brown the ground lamb in a non-stick pan over medium heat until fully cooked.
2. Mix the cooked lamb, quinoa, carrots, and green beans in a large pot.
3. Simmer the mixture over medium heat for 15 minutes or until the veggies are tender.
4. Let it cool before serving. If you're using olive oil, you can mix it in now.

This recipe offers an excellent source of protein from the lamb. The quinoa is a complete protein that provides a good fiber dose. The veggies add a burst of vitamins and minerals, and the optional olive oil is a source of healthy fats.

Frequent Small Meals: Easing the Load

The last leg of our culinary adventure brings us to meal frequency. As your dog's pregnancy progresses, her growing belly may make eating large meals uncomfortable. The solution? Offer her frequent, smaller meals throughout the day.

Think of it as a buffet. Instead of piling everything onto your plate in one go, you take a little bit of this, a little bit of that, and return for more when you're ready. This way, you can enjoy a variety of foods without overloading your plate (or, in this case, your dog's stomach).

Regular, small meals can aid in keeping blood sugar levels stable, guaranteeing a constant energy flow for your expecting dog and her developing puppies.

And there you have it! The recipe for success when feeding your pregnant and nursing dog: increased caloric intake, extra protein, and frequent, small meals. Adjusting your dog's diet during this particular time can give her the nutrients she needs to support her puppies' growth and maintain her health.

In the following chapters, we'll explore the fascinating world of homemade dog food, delving into health conditions, quick and easy meals, and even the delightful realm of doggie treats. So, tighten that apron and sharpen that chef's knife. Our culinary adventure is just getting started!

Golden Retrievers are sunshine-wrapped in fur, ready to turn your worst day into a festival of fetch and unconditional love. They're like living, breathing, slobbering reminders that every day is a good day for an adventure or a nap, depending on the snack situation.

4

COMBATTING CANINE HEALTH CHALLENGES THROUGH NUTRITION

L et's face it, we've all been there - that moment when you're enjoying a delicious meal and suddenly, out of the blue, you start itching, sneezing, or worse, your stomach decides to rebel. It's not a pleasant experience. Now, imagine your precious pooch going through the same ordeal. Yes, dogs, like humans, can also develop allergies to certain foods. But don't worry; I'm here to guide you on managing your dog's allergies through a specialized diet. Let's get started!

Managing Allergies with a Specialized Diet

Food allergies in dogs can appear in various ways, from persistent itching and skin infections to upset stomach and chronic diarrhea. If you've noticed these symptoms in your dog and your vet has confirmed a food allergy, it's time to consider changing your dog's diet. Here's how you can do it:

Grain-Free Recipes: A Simple Swap with Big Benefits

Certain dogs have allergies to grains such as wheat, corn, and soy. If your dog is one of them, switching to grain-free recipes can make a world of difference.

Here's a simple grain-free recipe you can try:

Beef and Sweet Potato Dinner

Serving Size:

- For small breeds (½ to 1 cup per meal), the recipe could provide around 7 to 14 servings.
- For medium breeds (1 to 2.5 cups per meal), it would yield approximately 3 to 7 servings.
- For large breeds (2.5 to 4 cups per meal), it might yield about 2 to 3 servings.

Ingredients:

- 2 pounds lean ground beef
- 2 sweet potatoes, diced
- 1 cup peas
- 1 tablespoon olive oil (optional)

Instructions:

1. Prepare the ground beef in a non-stick skillet on medium heat until thoroughly cooked.
2. Combine the cooked beef, sweet potatoes, and peas in a large pot.
3. Simmer the mixture over medium heat for about 15 minutes or until the sweet potatoes are tender.
4. Allow it to cool before serving. If you're using olive oil, you can stir it in now.

This recipe is not only grain-free but also packed with nutrients. The lean ground beef provides high-quality protein, while the sweet potatoes are a great source of fiber and vitamins. The peas add a touch of green and a boost of vitamins and minerals.

Novel Protein Recipes: A New Player in Town

If your dog is allergic to a specific type of protein - say, chicken or beef - introducing a novel protein can help. A novel protein is a type your dog has never eaten before, so your dog is less likely to be allergic to it. Examples include venison, rabbit, or duck.

Here's a simple recipe featuring duck, a novel protein:

Duck and Pumpkin Stew

Serving Size:

- For small breeds (½ to 1 cup per meal), the recipe could provide around 6 to 12 servings.
- For medium breeds (1 to 2.5 cups per meal), it would yield approximately 2.5 to 6 servings.
- For large breeds (2.5 to 4 cups per meal), it might yield about 1.5 to 3 servings.

Ingredients:

- 2 pounds of duck meat
- 2 cups of pumpkin puree
- 1 cup of green beans, chopped
- 1 tablespoon of fish oil (optional)

Instructions:

1. Cook the duck meat in a non-stick pan over medium heat until it's fully cooked.
2. Combine the cooked duck, pumpkin puree, and green beans in a large pot.
3. Simmer the mixture over medium heat for about 15 minutes or until the green beans are tender.
4. Let it cool before serving. If you're using fish oil, you can stir it in now.

This recipe is rich in novel protein from the duck and packed with fiber from the pumpkin. The green beans add a splash of color and a boost of vitamins. Simultaneously, the optional addition of fish oil provides a fantastic source of omega-3 fatty acids, beneficial in reducing inflammation associated with allergies.

Elimination Diet: Playing Detective with Your Dog's Diet

If your dog's allergies persist and you're unsure what's causing them, your vet may recommend an elimination diet. This involves feeding your dog a simple diet with minimal ingredients, then gradually reintroducing other foods while monitoring for allergic reactions.

To start an elimination diet, pick a protein and carbohydrate your dog has never eaten. For example, you might choose venison and sweet potatoes or salmon and peas. Feed your dog only these two ingredients for a few weeks, then reintroduce other foods one at a time and monitor their reaction.

Here's a basic elimination diet recipe:

Salmon and Peas Meal

Serving Size:

- For small breeds (½ to 1 cup per meal), the recipe could provide around 6 to 12 servings.
- For medium breeds (1 to 2.5 cups per meal), it would yield approximately 2.5 to 6 servings.
- For large breeds (2.5 to 4 cups per meal), it might yield about 1.5 to 3 servings.

Ingredients:

- 2 pounds fresh salmon fillets
- 2 cups of green peas
- 1 tablespoon of fish oil (optional)

Instructions:

1. Cook the salmon in a non-stick pan over medium heat until it's fully cooked.
2. In a large pot, combine the cooked salmon and peas.
3. Simmer the mixture over medium heat for about 15 minutes or until the peas are tender.
4. Let it cool before serving. If you're using fish oil, you can stir it in now.

Remember, an elimination diet should be conducted under your vet's supervision. Your veterinarian can guide you through the process and help you identify the foods causing your dog's allergies. Managing your dog's allergies through diet is like putting together a puzzle. It's about identifying the pieces - the foods that trigger your dog's allergies - and figuring out how to fit them together in a way that creates a complete, balanced, and allergen-free picture. It may seem challenging initially, but with patience, perseverance, and the proper guidance, you can help alleviate your dog's allergy symptoms and improve their quality of life. After all, there's no greater reward than seeing your furry friend happy, healthy, and itch-free!

Recipes for Dogs with Digestive Issues

The term 'digestive issues' covers a broad spectrum of conditions, from an upset tummy to chronic inflammatory bowel disease. Navigating this terrain can be like walking a tightrope. But with the proper diet, it's possible to maintain your dog's digestive health and keep them comfortable.

Probiotic Supplements: Friendly Bacteria to the Rescue

Probiotics, often called 'friendly bacteria,' can be a game-changer for dogs with digestive issues. They help balance your dog's gut flora, aiding digestion and keeping their immune system in check. Finding a good probiotic supplement for your dog involves some detective work. You must ensure the supplement has been tested for efficacy and safety. However, before adding any supplement to your dog's diet, it's wise to consult your vet.

Easily Digestible Foods: Light on the Tummy, Heavy on Nutrition

When feeding a dog with digestive issues, easily digestible foods are your best friend. Think of them as comfort food for your dog's tummy. These foods are gentle on the digestive system and provide the necessary nutrients without causing any upset.

Here's a simple recipe featuring easily digestible ingredients:

Chicken and Pumpkin Puree

Serving Size:

- For small breeds (½ to 1 cup per meal), the recipe could provide around 6 to 12 servings.

- For medium breeds (1 to 2.5 cups per meal), it would yield approximately 2.5 to 6 servings.
- For large breeds (2.5 to 4 cups per meal), it might yield about 1.5 to 3 servings.

Ingredients:

- 2 pounds of skinless chicken breast
- 2 cups of pumpkin puree
- 1 tablespoon of olive oil (optional)

Instructions:

1. Cook the chicken breast in a non-stick skillet over medium heat until it's fully cooked.
2. Mix the cooked chicken and pumpkin puree together in a large pot.
3. Simmer the mixture over medium heat for about 15 minutes or until thoroughly heated.
4. Let it cool before serving. If you're using olive oil, you can stir it in now.

This recipe is easy on the stomach and packed with nutrients. The chicken provides lean protein, while the pumpkin is a source of fiber and essential vitamins.

Small Frequent Meals: More Meals, Less Stress

Imagine you're at a buffet. You wouldn't pile everything onto your plate in one go, would you? Similarly, for dogs with digestive issues, more frequent, smaller meals can be easier on their system than one or two large meals a day.

By dividing your dog's daily food intake into four or five smaller meals, you can help prevent overloading their digestive system and decrease the frequency of digestive upset. Plus, your dog gets the excitement of mealtime more often throughout the day!

So, there you have it. With some friendly bacteria from probiotics, easily digestible foods, and smaller, more frequent meals, you can help manage your dog's digestive issues and keep its tail wagging. After all, a happy tummy means a happy dog!

But wait, our culinary adventure continues. We have more ground to cover, more recipes to explore, and more ways to tailor your dog's diet to their needs. So, let's keep going!

Dietary Support for Dogs with Heart Disease

Heart disease can be a scary diagnosis for any dog owner. But fear not, my fellow canine enthusiast, for we have the power of nutrition on our side. By tweaking your dog's diet and lifestyle, you can support their heart health and brighten their days. So, let's get right into it!

Low Sodium Recipes: An Ocean of Flavor without the Salt

First up, let's talk sodium. It's an essential mineral that helps balance your dog's body fluids. Nevertheless, excessive sodium intake can be detrimental, particularly for dogs suffering from heart disease. Excess sodium can cause fluid buildup, increasing the workload on a struggling heart. The answer to this problem? Low-sodium recipes!

Here's a heart-friendly, low-sodium recipe for your beloved pooch:

Turkey and Veggie Stir Fry

Serving Size:

- For small breeds (½ to 1 cup per meal), the recipe could provide around 7 to 14 servings.
- For medium breeds (1 to 2.5 cups per meal), it would yield approximately 3 to 7 servings.
- For large breeds (2.5 to 4 cups per meal), it might yield about 2 to 3 servings.

Ingredients:

- 2 pounds of ground turkey
- 2 sweet potatoes, diced
- 1 cup of spinach, chopped
- 1 tablespoon of olive oil (optional)

Instructions:

1. Cook the ground turkey in a non-stick pan over medium heat until it's fully cooked.
2. Combine the cooked turkey, sweet potatoes, and spinach in a large pot.
3. Simmer the mixture over medium heat for about 15 minutes or until the sweet potatoes are tender.
4. Let it cool before serving. If you're using olive oil, you can stir it in now.

This dish is low in sodium and has good nutrients for your dog's heart. The turkey provides lean protein, while the sweet potatoes are an excellent source of fiber and essential vitamins. The spinach adds a green touch and a boost of vitamins and minerals.

Omega-3 Fatty Acids: Fats That Love Your Dog's Heart

Next are omega-3 fatty acids. These fats have been shown to have heart health benefits for humans and canines. They help to reduce inflammation and can lower blood pressure, both of which are beneficial for dogs with heart disease.

Fish such as salmon and mackerel provide excellent sources of omega-3 fatty acids. You can include them in your dog's meals or consider a fish oil supplement. But before adding any supplement to your dog's diet, it's always a good idea to consult your vet. They can suggest the proper dosage based on your dog's weight and overall health.

Here's a recipe that's high in omega-3 fatty acids:

Salmon and Green Bean Medley

Serving Size:

- For small breeds (½ to 1 cup per meal), the recipe could provide around 6 to 12 servings.
- For medium breeds (1 to 2.5 cups per meal), it would yield approximately 2.5 to 6 servings.
- For large breeds (2.5 to 4 cups per meal), it might yield about 1.5 to 3 servings.

Ingredients:

- 2 pounds fresh salmon fillets
- 2 cups of green beans, chopped
- 1 tablespoon of fish oil (optional)

Instructions:

1. Cook the salmon in a non-stick pan over medium heat until it's fully cooked.
2. In a large pot, combine the cooked salmon and green beans.

3. Simmer the mixture over medium heat for about 15 minutes or until the green beans are tender.
4. Let it cool before serving. If you're using fish oil, you can stir it in now.

This recipe is a winner when it comes to omega-3 fatty acids. The salmon is a natural source of these heart-friendly fats, and the optional fish oil gives an extra boost. The green beans provide a bit of crunch and a dose of fiber and vitamins.

Regular Exercise: A Happy Heart is an Active Heart

Our final stop in this chapter is the exercise park. Just like us, dogs need consistent exercise to keep their hearts healthy. For a dog with heart disease, regular, gentle exercise can help to strengthen their heart muscle and improve circulation.

But remember, the goal isn't to turn your dog into an athlete. It's about keeping them active and enjoying life. Gentle walks, short play sessions, and plenty of rest are the order of the day.

So, that's it! With low-sodium recipes, omega-3 fatty acids, and regular exercise, you can provide the dietary support your dog needs to manage their heart disease. You're not just their best friend but their heart health hero!

Nutritional Strategies for Weight Management

Now, let's switch gears and talk about weight management. Whether your dog needs to ditch a few pounds or maintain their current weight, the proper diet can make all the difference. So, let's dig into some strategies that can help keep your dog's weight in check.

Low-Calorie Recipes: Big on Taste, Light on Calories

The first tool in your weight management toolkit is low-calorie recipes. These are meals that are high in nutrients but low in calories. They allow your dog to feel full and satisfied without the extra calories that can lead to weight gain.

Here's a low-calorie recipe to try:

Chicken and Zucchini Stir Fry

Serving Size:

- For small breeds (½ to 1 cup per meal), the recipe could provide around 6 to 12 servings.
- For medium breeds (1 to 2.5 cups per meal), it would yield approximately 2.5 to 6 servings.
- For large breeds (2.5 to 4 cups per meal), it might yield about 1.5 to 3 servings.

Ingredients:

- 2 pounds of skinless chicken breast
- 2 zucchinis, diced
- 1 tablespoon of olive oil (optional)

Instructions:

1. Cook the chicken breast in a non-stick skillet over medium heat until it's fully cooked.
2. Combine the cooked chicken and diced zucchini in a large pot.
3. Simmer the mixture over medium heat for about 15 minutes or until the zucchinis are tender.
4. Let it cool before serving. If you're using olive oil, you can stir it in now.

This recipe is not only low in calories but also packed with nutrients. The chicken provides lean protein, while the zucchinis offer an excellent source of fiber and essential vitamins.

One More Recipe for Weight Management

Lean Cuisine for Canine Companions

Let's face it, we all know that a slice of chocolate cake has more calories than a bowl of salad. And while we might choose the cake (because, yum!), when it comes to our four-legged friends, we need to make choices that will keep them healthy, at an ideal weight, and alive. Here's another low-calorie recipe that will keep your dog's tail wagging without packing on the pounds.

Turkey and Carrot Delight

Serving Size:

- For small breeds (½ to 1 cup per meal), the recipe could provide around 6 to 12 servings.
- For medium breeds (1 to 2.5 cups per meal), it would yield approximately 2.5 to 6 servings.
- For large breeds (2.5 to 4 cups per meal), it might yield about 1.5 to 3 servings.

Ingredients:

- 2 pounds of ground turkey
- 2 cups of carrots, diced
- 1 tablespoon of coconut oil (optional)

Instructions:

1. Cook the ground turkey in a non-stick pan over medium heat until fully cooked.
2. In a large pot, mix the cooked turkey and diced carrots.
3. Simmer the mixture over medium heat for about 15 minutes or until the carrots are soft.
4. Let it cool before serving. If you're using coconut oil, you can mix it in now.

This recipe is a hit with dogs and is light on calories. Ground turkey provides lean protein, while carrots are low-calorie and rich in fiber and vitamins.

The Portion Puzzle: Getting it Just Right

Now that we have our low-calorie recipe let's talk about portion control. This is a critical player in managing your dog's weight. Here's the thing: Even the healthiest foods can contribute to weight gain if your dog overeats.

How do we figure out the right portion size for our dogs? It's easier than it might sound. A simple way to gauge the right portion size is by using a measuring cup. This can help you be sure your dog gets the right amount of food based on size and activity level.

Remember, these are just guidelines. Each dog is unique, and their feeding needs vary based on breed, age, and overall health. So, it's always a good idea to consult with your vet, who can give personalized advice on portion sizes for your dog.

Exercise: A Walk in the Park

We've covered the dietary aspects of weight management, and now, let's step into the world of physical activity. Consistent exercise is critical for maintaining a healthy weight in dogs. It helps them burn those extra calories and keeps their joints flexible and their minds active.

Before training your dog for a marathon, remember that the goal is regular, moderate exercise. A daily walk or fetch can be just the ticket for keeping your dog active and at a healthy weight.

The amount of exercise your fourlegged friend requires can depend on their breed, age, and health status. Always remember to keep the exercise sessions enjoyable for your dog. After all, a happy dog is an active dog!

So, there you have it, folks! With these low-calorie recipes, portion control tips, and exercise ideas, you can help your dog maintain a healthy weight. Remember, it's not about depriving them of food or pushing them to exercise excessively. It's about creating a balanced lifestyle that keeps them healthy and happy. Because, at the end of the day, our dogs aren't just pets; they're family, and they deserve the best care we can provide. So, on to the next chapter of our culinary adventure!

Rottweilers are the bouncers of the dog world, with a heart of gold hidden beneath their tough exterior. They're like living, breathing security systems that will love you fiercely and might drool on intruders as a warning. Always ready for a belly rub just after they've checked your ID.

5

FAST AND FLAVORFUL: QUICK HOMEMADE DOG FOOD RECIPES

Picture this: It's been a bustling day, full of errands, meetings, and the usual whirlwind of life's responsibilities. Your dog, who has been patiently waiting, looks up at you with those adoring eyes, tail wagging in anticipation of dinner. You want to provide a nutritious, homemade meal, but your energy levels are waning, and the clock is ticking. Sound familiar? Don't worry, you're not alone. We've all had those days when time runs fast, like a Greyhound on a race track.

This chapter is your lifeline for those time-crunched moments. It's all about quick, easy-to-prepare, yet nutritionally balanced recipes that satisfy your dog's appetite and your desire for convenience. These recipes are designed to be prepared in 30 minutes or less, making them perfect for hectic weekdays or when you need a quick and easy meal option. Ready to discover the world of fast and flavorful dog cuisine? Let's dive in!

Chicken and Vegetable Medley

Imagine a colorful medley of nutritious vegetables simmering with tender chicken, filling your kitchen with a mouthwatering aroma with your dog spinning in joyous circles. This recipe is not only a visual treat, but it's also packed with essential nutrients.

Serving Size:

- For small breeds (½ to 1 cup per meal), the recipe could provide around 4 to 12 servings.
- For medium breeds (1 to 2.5 cups per meal), it would yield approximately 2 to 6 servings.
- For large breeds (2.5 to 4 cups per meal), it might yield about 1 to 2 servings.

Ingredients:

- 1 chicken breast
- 1 cup carrots
- 1 cup green beans
- 1 cup sweet potatoes

Recipe Time:

1. Start with boiling a chicken breast. While it's simmering, take this time to chop up your vegetables. Dice the carrots, slice the green beans, and cube the sweet potatoes. This medley of vegetables will provide a variety of vitamins and minerals, all necessary for your dog's health.
2. Remove the chicken from the pot and let it cool once it is fully cooked. Do not throw away the broth. It's packed with flavor and nutrients and will be used to cook the vegetables.
3. Add your chopped veggies to the pot with the chicken broth and let them simmer until tender. This process should take

   10-15 minutes, depending on how small you've chopped
   them.
4. While the veggies are cooking, shred the cooled chicken into
   bite-sized pieces. Check for any small bones that might have
   been missed.
5. Once the veggies are cooked, mix in the shredded chicken.
   Let it cool down before serving it to your eager pup.

And voila! In less than 30 minutes, you have a nutritious, homemade
meal without fancy ingredients or hours in the kitchen. The chicken
provides lean protein, the carrots and sweet potatoes are excellent
sources of beta-carotene and fiber, and the green beans add a nice
crunch that many dogs love.

This recipe can be adjusted easily based on
what you have in your pantry. No green
beans? No problem. You can use peas, broc-
coli, or any other dog-safe vegetable.
Remember, variety is the spice of life and the
key to a balanced diet. So, don't hesitate to
mix things up and keep your dog's meals
exciting and nutritious.

You can still provide your dog a healthy, homemade meal. With some
planning, simple ingredients, and a dash of love, you can whip up a
delicious meal that will have your dog licking the bowl clean. So,
remember this recipe the next time you need more time. It may
become your go-to for a quick, nutritious dog meal.

By introducing your dog to the flavors of homemade food, you're
doing more than just feeding them. You're taking an active role in
their health, showing them love in a way that also benefits their well-
being, and creating mealtime memories that you'll both cherish. So,
keep that apron handy and those pots ready. Your journey into the
world of homemade dog food is just getting started.

Beef Stew for Dogs

Imagine this: a simmering pot of hearty beef stew, the aroma filling your kitchen, making your stomach rumble and your dog's tail wag in anticipation. This hearty dish isn't just for you. It is a nutritious and delicious meal for your furry friend with a few tweaks. So, let's roll up our sleeves and get cooking!

Serving Size:

- For small breeds (½ to 1 cup per meal), the recipe could provide around 6 to 16 servings.
- For medium breeds (1 to 2.5 cups per meal), it would yield approximately 2.5 to 6 servings.
- For large breeds (2.5 to 4 cups per meal), it might yield about 1.5 to 3 servings.

Ingredients:

- 1 pound lean ground beef
- 1 cup kidney beans
- 1 cup carrots
- 1 cup butternut squash

Turning these simple ingredients into a meal your dog will love is easier than you might think. It's all about combining them in the right way, at the right time, to create a dish rich in flavor and loaded with nutrients.

Recipe Time:

1. Start by browning the ground beef in a large pot over medium heat. You don't need any oil as the meat will let its juices out as it cooks. Break up the beef into bite-sized pieces that are better for your dog to chew and digest.

2. Prepare your vegetables while the beef is cooking, and peel and dice the butternut squash and carrots into small cubes. Remember, smaller pieces are more accessible for your dog to eat and digest. Plus, they cook faster, saving you time.

3. After the beef is fully cooked, add the diced vegetables to the pot. Stir everything together to ensure the vegetables are coated in the beef's juices. This will give them extra flavor that your dog will love.

4. Next, rinse your kidney beans in cold water to remove excess sodium. Then, add them to the pot. Kidney beans are good for fiber and plant-based protein. However, use kidney beans sparingly as too many can cause digestive upset in dogs.

5. Cover the pot and let everything simmer on medium heat for about 20 minutes or until the vegetables are tender. Be sure to stir occasionally to prevent anything from sticking to the bottom of the pot.

And that's it! You've prepared a hearty beef stew for your dog in about half an hour. Let it cool before serving to avoid burning your dog's mouth.

This beef stew isn't just tasty; it's also tailored to your dog's nutritional needs. Lean ground beef is a source of quality protein essential for maintaining your dog's muscles and overall body function.

The carrots and butternut squash provide a variety of vitamins and minerals. Carrots are high in beta-carotene, which is good for your dog's eyesight. Butternut squash is packed with fiber, aiding digestion. It is also a great source of vitamin A, vitamin C, and potassium.

Lastly, the kidney beans, while a more minor part of the meal, offer a plant-based protein source and are rich in fiber, helping to keep your dog's digestive system running smoothly.

Remember, variety is good when it comes to your dog's diet. Feel free to substitute other dog-safe vegetables or switch out the beef for another protein source. The goal is to provide a balanced, nutritious meal that caters to your dog's specific needs and preferences. So, feel free to get creative and try different combinations. Your dog will thank you for it!

Feeding your dog can be manageable, even on the busiest days. With recipes like this, you can provide your dog with the nutritious, home-made meals they deserve without spending hours in the kitchen. So, remember this recipe the next time you need more time. Who knows? This beef stew might just become your dog's new favorite meal!

Fish Delight: Salmon and Peas

Ah, the humble salmon. This pink-hued fish isn't just a restaurant favorite; it's also a powerhouse of nutrition, making it a fantastic ingredient for your dog's meals. Add in some green peas and sweet potatoes, drizzle some olive oil, and you've got a delicious, nutritious meal that your dog will love.

Serving Size:

- For small breeds (½ to 1 cup per meal), the recipe could provide around 4 to 12 servings.
- For medium breeds (1 to 2.5 cups per meal), it would yield approximately 2 to 6 servings.
- For large breeds (2.5 to 4 cups per meal), it might yield about 1 to 2 servings.

Ingredients:

- 1 pound fresh salmon fillets
- 1 cup green peas
- 1 cup sweet potatoes

- 1 tablespoon olive oil

Recipe Time:

1. Begin by cooking the fresh salmon fillets in a non-stick pan over medium heat. There's no need to add oil, as the salmon will release its juices. Cook the fillets until they are opaque and flake easily with a fork. After it's cooked, remove the salmon from the pan and let it cool.
2. As the salmon cools down, cook the peas and sweet potatoes. Peel the sweet potatoes and chop them into small, bite-sized pieces. Add the diced sweet potatoes and green peas to a pot of boiling water. Boil them until tender, which should take about 10-15 minutes.
3. You can flake the salmon into small, bite-sized pieces once the salmon has cooled down. Be sure to check for any small bones and remove them.
4. Drain the cooked peas and sweet potatoes, then combine them with the flaked salmon in a large bowl. Stir everything together until it's well mixed.
5. To finish, drizzle a tablespoon of olive oil over the mixture. Olive oil adds some extra flavor and is a tremendous source of omega-3 fatty acids that benefit your dog's skin and coat health.
6. Before serving your dog, let the meal cool down. This will prevent potential burns and make the meal more enjoyable for your dog.

And there it is—a quick, easy, and nutritious meal that's sure to delight your dog's taste buds.

Salmon is a fantastic source of quality protein essential for maintaining your dog's muscle mass and overall body function. It also provides omega-3 fatty acids, which support skin and coat health, provide anti-inflammatory benefits, and even aid in brain development in puppies.

Green peas are a source of plant-based protein. They contain vitamins and minerals, including vitamins A, K, and B6. They also provide dietary fiber, which aids digestion and helps to keep your dog feeling full.

Sweet potatoes, on the other hand, are a source of dietary fiber, vitamin C, and beta-carotene. They're also low in fat, making them an excellent ingredient for dogs watching their weight.

Finally, a drizzle of olive oil adds extra flavor. It contains a dose of healthy fats and vitamin E, contributing to a shiny coat and healthier skin for your dog.

Preparing homemade meals for your dog doesn't have to be a time-consuming chore. With recipes like this, you can whip up a healthy and delicious meal in no time. And the best part? Knowing what's in your dog's bowl gives you peace of mind. So, what are you waiting for? Grab that apron, fire up that stove, and try this recipe. Your dog will thank you for it!

Turkey and Brown Rice Dinner: A Nutrient-Rich Feast

Envision a steaming bowl of ground turkey, fluffy brown rice, and colorful vegetables. It's a sight to behold. Imagine your dog's delight as they dig into this nutritious, delectable feast. This meal isn't just about tantalizing your dog's taste buds; it's about providing them with a balanced, nutrient-rich meal that supports their overall health. Ready to turn this dream into reality? Let's get cooking!

Serving Size:

- For small breeds (½ to 1 cup per meal), the recipe could provide around 6 to 12 servings.

- For medium breeds (1 to 2.5 cups per meal), it would yield approximately 2.5 to 6 servings.
- For large breeds (2.5 to 4 cups per meal), it might yield about 1.5 to 3 servings.

Ingredients:

- 1 pound ground turkey
- 2 cups brown rice
- 1 cup spinach
- 1 cup carrots
- 1 cup zucchini

Recipe Time:

1. Begin with the centerpiece of our meal - the ground turkey. Cook it in a non-stick skillet over medium heat until it's well-cooked. Ground turkey contains lean protein. It is crucial for maintaining your dog's muscles and supporting their overall body function.
2. While the turkey is sizzling away, let's focus on the brown rice. Cook it according to the package instructions. Remember, we're going for fluffy, not mushy. Brown rice provides sources of complex carbohydrates, giving your dog energy to be active and playful.
3. Now, onto the veggies. Chop the spinach, carrots, and zucchini into bite-sized pieces. These fresh vegetables add a pop of color to our meals and bring a host of vitamins and minerals to the table.
4. Once the turkey is cooked, combine it with the cooked brown rice and chopped vegetables in a large pot. Stir everything together until well mixed.
5. Allow the meal to cool before serving it to your dog. This ensures your dog can enjoy the meal without the risk of burning its mouth.

And there you go - a nutritious, homemade meal that's quick to prepare and sure to be a hit with your dog.

This recipe is more than just a tasty meal; it's a carefully crafted blend of nutrients. The ground turkey provides lean protein, the brown rice offers slow-releasing energy, and the colorful vegetables combine vitamins and minerals into your dog's bowl.

Feeding your dog doesn't have to be a time-consuming task. With recipes like this, you can provide a wholesome, homemade meal that caters to your dog's nutritional needs and your busy schedule. So, remember this recipe the next time you're wondering what to feed your dog. It's quick, easy, and sure to get your dog's tail wagging.

With every meal you prepare and every ingredient you select, you're doing more than just feeding your dog; you're nourishing them. You're taking an active role in their health and well-being. It's a labor of love that will deepen your bond with your furry friend. So, keep those pots simmering and your dog's taste buds guessing with the variety of recipes you now have in your arsenal.

Now, as we move forward, we'll turn our attention to the art of creating homemade meals for your dog that don't just cater to their nutritional needs but also your budget. So, stay tuned as we jump into the world of budget-friendly homemade dog food recipes!

Beagles are the Houdinis of the canine world, able to escape from any yard with the promise of adventure — or just an exciting smell. They're like four-legged detectives with floppy ears, always on the case of the next great scent, leading them to the most unexpected places, like your sandwich.

6

FEEDING FIDO ON A BUDGET: COST-EFFECTIVE HOMEMADE RECIPES

L ife is full of surprises. Sometimes, they're pleasant, like finding a forgotten $20 bill in your pocket. Other times, they're unpleasant, like getting an unexpected bill in the mail. As much as we love our canine companions, the cost of providing for them can sometimes be a surprise. This chapter is about changing that. It's about taking control of your dog's diet without breaking the bank. It's about proving that you don't need to be a millionaire to feed your dog a healthy, homemade diet. So, let's crunch those numbers and get cooking!

Hearty Ground Turkey Mix

Think of a steaming bowl of ground turkey mixed with fluffy brown rice and a colorful medley of vegetables. It's a sight to behold. But what if I told you that this hearty meal is nutritious for your dog and easy on your wallet? That's right, my fellow dog devotees. Feeding your dog a homemade diet doesn't have to cost a fortune. Here's a budget-friendly recipe with your dog's tail wagging and your wallet sighing in relief.

Serving Size:

- For small breeds (½ to 1 cup per meal), the recipe could provide around 6 to 12 servings.
- For medium breeds (1 to 2.5 cups per meal), it would yield approximately 2.5 to 6 servings.
- For large breeds (2.5 to 4 cups per meal), it might yield about 1.5 to 3 servings.

Ingredients:

- 1 pound ground turkey
- 2 cups brown rice
- 1 cup mixed vegetables

Recipe Time:

1. Start by cooking the ground turkey in a non-stick pan over medium heat. You don't need any oil, as the turkey will release its juices. This lean protein source is suitable for your dog's health. It is relatively inexpensive, especially if you buy it in bulk.
2. You can prepare the brown rice while the turkey is cooking. This grain is an excellent source of slow-releasing energy and is also kind to your budget. Cook the rice as the package instructions suggest, and fluff it with a fork once it's done.
3. Now, let's talk veggies. Frozen mixed vegetables are a real game-changer here. They're not only cheaper than fresh vegetables, but they're also a real-time-saver as they're already cleaned, chopped, and ready to use. Plus, they're flash-frozen at the peak of their freshness, so they retain their nutritional value.
4. Once the turkey is fully cooked and the rice is fluffy, combine them in a large pot with the frozen vegetables. You can heat

the mixture over medium heat for about 5-10 minutes until the vegetables are heated through.

5. Let the meal cool before serving it to your eager pooch.

And just like that—a budget-friendly, nutritionally balanced meal that didn't take hours to prepare or cost a fortune. The ground turkey provides the protein your dog needs for healthy muscles, the brown rice provides the carbohydrates they need for energy, and the mixed vegetables offer a wide range of vitamins and minerals. It's a win-win for you and your furry friend!

As you can see, feeding your dog a homemade diet doesn't have to be a costly endeavor. With intelligent ingredient choices and budget-friendly recipes like this, you can provide your dog with the nutritious, homemade meals they deserve without straining your budget. So, embrace the challenge, experiment with different ingredients, and discover the joy of creating healthy, affordable meals for your dog. After all, good nutrition isn't a luxury; it's a necessity. And every dog, regardless of their owner's budget, deserves to enjoy a diet that supports their health and well-being.

Tips to Make this Recipe Even More Budget-Friendly:

Here are a few tips to keep your budget in check:

- Buy ingredients in bulk: Purchasing larger quantities can often save costs. Plus, having these staples on hand makes it easier to prepare meals on the fly.
- Use store-brand products: Store brands often offer the same quality as name brands but at a better deal.
- Look for sales and discounts: Keep an eye on your local grocery store's sales and deals. You might find your dog's favorite ingredients at a reduced price.

Embrace the challenge, enjoy the process, and remember, the goal is to provide your dog with a healthy diet that fits comfortably within your budget. So, stay tuned for more budget-friendly recipes, tips, and tricks to help you master the art of homemade dog food without breaking the bank.

Chicken and Pumpkin Stew: A Bounty of Flavor on a Budget

How about a cozy, comforting stew that's easy on the pocket and a cornucopia of nutrition for your four-legged companion? Let's turn to our main characters for this recipe - chicken thighs, pumpkin puree, green beans, and carrots.

Serving Size:

- For small breeds (½ to 1 cup per meal), the recipe could provide around 6 to 12 servings.
- For medium breeds (1 to 2.5 cups per meal), it would yield approximately 2.5 to 6 servings.
- For large breeds (2.5 to 4 cups per meal), it might yield about 1.5 to 3 servings.

Ingredients:

- 1 pound chicken thighs
- 1 cup pumpkin puree
- 1 cup green beans
- 1 cup carrots

Recipe Time:

1. Initiate this culinary creation by focusing on the chicken thighs. Opt for skinless and boneless ones to ensure your dog doesn't ingest any small bones, which could present a choking hazard. Brown the chicken thighs in a large, non-

stick pan over medium heat. There's no need for additional oil or fat since the thighs naturally contain enough fat to prevent sticking.

2. As the chicken cooks, shift your attention to the vegetables. Opt for fresh green beans and carrots, which are economical and brimming with essential nutrients. Rinse them under cold water, then chop them into bite-sized pieces, ensuring they're small enough for your dog to safely chew and swallow.

3. Once the chicken thighs are thoroughly cooked, set them aside to cool. This is essential as it prevents your dog from burning their mouth on hot food. While the chicken is cooling, you can cook the vegetables. Place the green beans and carrots in a pot of boiling water and let them simmer until tender. This should take about 10-15 minutes.

4. While the vegetables are cooking, let's follow up on the chicken. Now that it's cool, you can chop it into small, bite-sized pieces, ensuring no bones or skin are left behind.

5. Drain the cooked vegetables, then combine them with the chopped chicken in a large bowl. Add a generous dollop of pumpkin puree to the mix. Canned pumpkin puree is a budget-friendly ingredient with fiber, vitamin A, and other beneficial nutrients.

6. Mix everything, ensuring the pumpkin puree coats the chicken and vegetables evenly. The result is a hearty stew that's delicious and rich in protein, fiber, and essential vitamins and minerals.

And presto, a budget-friendly, nutritionally balanced meal that's quick to whip up and sure to have your dog licking their bowl clean. The chicken thighs provide a cost-effective source of protein. At the same time, pumpkin puree, green beans, and carrots contribute fiber, vitamins, and minerals. Plus, the pumpkin adds a sweetness that many dogs find irresistible.

As you can see, homemade dog food doesn't have to come with a hefty price tag. With some resourcefulness and creativity, you can whip up nutritious, tasty meals with your dog's tail wagging in delight without straining your budget.

So, the next time you're at the supermarket, remember this recipe. Those chicken thighs and that can of pumpkin puree could be the start of your dog's next favorite meal that's good for their health and kind to your wallet. Isn't that a delicious thought?

Remember, the goal isn't to create gourmet meals or impress with fancy ingredients. It's about providing your dog with homemade food that supports their health and fits comfortably within your budget. And with recipes like these, you're well on your way to achieving that goal.

So, keep those pots simmering and your dog's taste buds guessing with the variety of recipes you now have in your culinary repertoire. With every meal you prepare, you're taking an active role in your dog's health, showing them love in a way that benefits their well-being.

Ready for more? Our next recipe will explore an additional budget-friendly recipe with tips and tricks to help you navigate the world of homemade dog food even more.

Beef and Quinoa Meal

Now imagine a simmering pot of lean ground beef, quinoa, peas, and carrots, filling your kitchen with an aroma with your dog spinning in joyous circles. This dish isn't just for you. It becomes a nutritious and delicious meal for your canine companion with a few tweaks. Ready to make this vision a reality? Let's start!

Serving Size:

- For small breeds (½ to 1 cup per meal), the recipe could provide around 6 to 12 servings.
- For medium breeds (1 to 2.5 cups per meal), it would yield approximately 2.5 to 6 servings.
- For large breeds (2.5 to 4 cups per meal), it might yield about 1.5 to 3 servings.

Ingredients:

- 1 pound lean ground beef
- 2 cups quinoa
- 1 cup peas
- 1 cup carrots

Recipe Time:

1. Start with the star of our meal - the lean ground beef. Brown it in a non-stick pan over medium heat. No need for any oil as the beef will release its own juices. Ground beef is not only a crowd-pleaser when it comes to taste, but it's also rich in protein, iron, and B vitamins.
2. While the beef is cooking, get started on the quinoa. Rinse it under cold water to remove any bitter outer coating, then cook it according to package instructions. Quinoa is a super grain that's not only budget-friendly but also packed with protein and fiber.
3. Now, onto the veggies. Rinse the peas and dice the carrots. These veggies will provide a variety of textures, colors, and, more importantly, a bounty of vitamins and minerals.
4. Once the beef is fully cooked, mix it with the cooked quinoa, peas, and diced carrots in a large bowl. Stir everything together to ensure the ingredients are evenly distributed.
5. Allow the meal to cool before serving it to your furry friend. This will prevent potential burns and make the meal more enjoyable for your canine companion.

In just about 30 minutes, you've prepared a hearty meal that's tasty, nutritionally balanced, and easy on your budget.

In the grand scheme of things, preparing homemade meals for your dog is one small step for you but a giant leap for your dog's health. It's about making the choice to feed your dog food that's not only nutritious but also wallet-friendly.

So, the next time you're at the market, remember this recipe. A packet of lean ground beef, a box of quinoa, a bag of peas, and a few carrots are all you need to create a healthy, homemade meal that's sure to get your dog's tail wagging.

Stay tuned for one more budget-friendly recipe with tips and tricks to help you navigate the world of homemade dog food without breaking the bank. After all, good nutrition isn't a luxury; it's a necessity. And every dog, regardless of their owner's budget, deserves to enjoy a diet that supports their health and well-being. So, let's make it happen, one homemade meal at a time!

Sweet Potato and Fish Feast

Who says you can't have a feast on a budget? Picture this: succulent white fish fillets, naturally sweet and creamy sweet potatoes, vibrant green beans, all brought together with a drizzle of olive oil. This isn't just a meal; it's a feast fit for your four-legged king or queen. And the best part? It's budget-friendly, simple to prepare, and packed with nutrients. Ready for this dream to come true? Let's begin!

Serving Size:

- For small breeds (½ to 1 cup per meal), the recipe could provide around 6 to 12 servings.
- For medium breeds (1 to 2.5 cups per meal), it would yield approximately 2.5 to 6 servings.

- For large breeds (2.5 to 4 cups per meal), it might yield about 1.5 to 3 servings.

Ingredients:

- 1 pound white fish fillets
- 2 cups sweet potatoes
- 1 cup green beans
- 1 tablespoon olive oil

Recipe Time:

1. Hop on the cooking express by focusing on the star of our meal - the white fish fillets. Cook the fillets in a non-stick skillet over medium heat. No need for any oil as the fish will release its oils. Whitefish is not only a hit when it comes to taste but is also brimming with lean protein and Omega-3 fatty acids.
2. While the fish is cooking, turn your attention to the sweet potatoes. Peel and dice them into bite-sized pieces. Sweet potatoes are a cost-effective ingredient that brings a load of fiber, vitamins, and minerals to your dog's bowl.
3. Next, let's tackle the green beans. Finely chop the green beans. These vibrant veggies add a sprinkle of color to our meals and serve a host of beneficial nutrients, including fiber, Vitamin C, and Vitamin K.
4. Once the fish fillets are fully cooked, remove them from the pan and let them cool. This is crucial to avoid any potential burns when serving the meal to your dog. While the fish is cooling, you can cook the sweet potatoes and green beans. Add them to a pot of boiling water and let them simmer until tender. This should take about 10-15 minutes.
5. Flake the fish into small, bite-sized pieces when it is cooled, ensuring no bones are left behind.

6. Drain the cooked sweet potatoes and green beans, then mix them with the flaked fish in a large bowl.
7. To finish, drizzle a tablespoon of olive oil over the mixture. Olive oil contains healthy fats and can contribute to a shiny coat and healthier skin for your dog.
8. Allow the meal to cool down before serving it to your dog. This ensures your dog can enjoy the meal without the risk of burning its mouth.

And there's the magic! A budget-friendly, nutritionally balanced meal that's quick to prepare and full of flavors that your dog will love. The white fish provides lean protein and Omega-3 fatty acids, the sweet potatoes offer a great source of fiber and vitamins, and the green beans add a dash of green and a dose of vitamins.

Embracing a homemade diet for your dog doesn't mean you have to say goodbye to convenience or wreck your budget. With some planning, simple ingredients, and a handful of easy-to-follow recipes, you can whip up nutritious, tasty meals that your dog will love.

So, don't forget this recipe the next time you plan your grocery list. A few white fish fillets, a couple of sweet potatoes, a handful of green beans, and a dash of olive oil are all you need to create a nutritious, homemade meal that's easy on your budget and sure to get your dog's mouth-watering.

Feeding your dog a homemade diet is about more than just nutrition. It's about the love that goes into preparing each meal, the peace of mind from knowing exactly what's in your dog's bowl, and the joy of seeing your dog's excitement at mealtime. And with recipes like this, you can experience all of this without straining your budget.

So, keep your pots ready, your pantry stocked, and your dog's tummy happy with the variety of budget-friendly recipes you now have. With each meal you prepare, you're not just feeding your dog; you're nourishing them, showing them love, and investing in their health and well-being.

As we journey forward, we'll continue to explore the world of homemade dog food, diving into grain-free recipes for dogs with sensitive tummies in our next chapter. With the correct information, a handful of recipes, and a dash of determination, we can provide our dogs with the nutritious, delicious meals they deserve, all within the confines of our budget. Together, let's prove that good nutrition is not just a luxury for the few but a right for all dogs. So, let's turn the page and continue our budget-friendly culinary adventure!

Dachshunds are the original low-riders of the dog world, with a bark more significant than their bite and a body that looks like it's been stretched for comedic effect. They're adorable, sausage-shaped warriors, fiercely loyal and always ready to tunnel into the coziest blanket fort or your heart, whichever is closer.

SHARE YOUR JOURNEY

Halfway through **Easy and Healthy Homemade Dog Food Recipes and Guide**, I hope it's been enlightening and inspiring. Your dedication to your dog's health through nutritious, homemade meals is admirable. If you've found this guide valuable, please share your feedback on **Amazon**. Your review could help other pet owners discover the benefits of homemade dog food. Your experiences and insights are vital to our community of conscientious pet owners, aiding others in their journey to healthier, happier dogs. Thank you for your support and for joining this journey.

Scan the QR Code to Leave Your Review

FREE COLOR IMAGES AND FREE TRANSITION GUIDE

To Access FREE-Color Images of Recipes and Your FREE 31-Day Transition Guide, Scan the QR Code Below

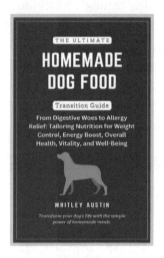

7

GRAIN-FREE GOODNESS: NOURISHING RECIPES FOR SENSITIVE TUMMIES

E ver tried a new food and ended up with a grumbling tummy? It's uncomfortable. Now, imagine your beloved furry friend going through the same ordeal. Yes, dogs, like humans, can also develop sensitivities or allergies to certain grains. But worry not, my fellow dog devotees! This chapter is all about grain-free recipes that are gentle on your dog's stomach yet rich in nutrition and flavor. Let's delve straight into our grain-free culinary adventure!

Chicken and Sweet Potato Grain-Free Dinner

Let's start with a simple, nutritious recipe combining lean chicken breast, sweet potatoes, green beans, and a drizzle of olive oil. This combination tastes great and provides a balanced meal for your dog. Let's break it down:

Serving Size:

- For small breeds (½ to 1 cup per meal), the recipe could provide around 6 to 12 servings.

- For medium breeds (1 to 2.5 cups per meal), it would yield approximately 2.5 to 6 servings.
- For large breeds (2.5 to 4 cups per meal), it might yield about 1.5 to 3 servings.

Ingredients:

- 1 pound chicken breast
- 2 cups sweet potatoes
- 1 cup green beans
- 1 tablespoon olive oil

Recipe Time:

1. Begin by cooking the chicken breast in a non-stick pan over medium heat. Once it's fully cooked, remove it from the pan and let it cool. This is essential as it prevents your dog from burning their mouth on hot food. Chicken breast is a lean protein, crucial for maintaining your dog's muscles and supporting their overall body function.
2. As the chicken is cooling, you can prepare the sweet potatoes. Finely dice them and add them to a pot of boiling water. Let them simmer until they're tender. This should take about 10-15 minutes. Sweet potatoes are not only naturally sweet and delicious, but they're also a great source of dietary fiber, vitamin A, and other essential nutrients.
3. Next, let's tackle the green beans. These vibrant veggies add color to our meal and serve a host of beneficial nutrients, including fiber, Vitamin C, and Vitamin K. Rinse the green beans under cold water, then chop them into bite-sized pieces. Add the beans to the pot with the sweet potatoes for the last 5 minutes of cooking.
4. Now that your chicken has cooled, you can chop it into small, bite-sized pieces. This ensures that no large chunks could pose a choking hazard for your dog.

5. Once all your ingredients are prepared, it's time to assemble your meal. Combine the chopped chicken, cooked sweet potatoes, and green beans in a large bowl. Stir everything together until it's well mixed.
6. To finish, drizzle a tablespoon of olive oil over the mixture. Healthy fats are in olive oil and benefit your dog's skin and coat health. Plus, it adds some extra flavor that your dog will love.
7. Allow the meal to cool before serving it to your eager dog. This ensures your dog can enjoy the meal without the risk of burns.

And thus, the masterpiece is revealed! A grain-free, nutritionally balanced meal that's quick to prepare and sure to be a hit with your dog. The chicken provides lean protein, the sweet potatoes offer a great source of fiber and vitamins, and the green beans add a dash of green and a dose of vitamins.

Feeding your dog a grain-free diet doesn't mean you have to compromise on flavor or nutrition. With recipes like this, you can provide your dog with the wholesome, homemade meals they deserve while catering to their dietary needs. So, the next time you're planning your dog's dinner, remember this recipe. It's quick, easy, and sure to get your dog's tail wagging.

As you continue to explore grain-free recipes for your dog, gradually introduce new foods and monitor your dog for any signs of digestive upset. Every dog is unique, and what works for one may not work for another. The key is to find recipes that suit your dog's specific needs and preferences. So, don't be afraid to experiment with different ingredients and create grain-free recipes. After all, the best meals are those made with love and tailored to the ones we care for.

Stay tuned as we continue to explore grain-free recipes for your dog. In the coming sections, we'll uncover more delicious and nutritious recipes that are easy on your dog's stomach and packed with the nutrients they need to thrive. So, let's keep those pots simmering, those tails wagging, and our journey toward healthier, happier dogs going strong!

Beef and Veggie Grain-Free Meal

Serving Size:

- For small breeds (½ to 1 cup per meal), the recipe could provide around 6 to 12 servings.
- For medium breeds (1 to 2.5 cups per meal), it would yield approximately 2.5 to 6 servings.
- For large breeds (2.5 to 4 cups per meal), it might yield about 1.5 to 3 servings.

Ingredients:

- 1 pound lean ground beef
- 2 cups butternut squash
- 1 cup carrots
- 1 cup peas

Recipe Time:

1. Every tasty meal starts with quality ingredients, and the spotlight is on lean ground beef for this dish. Begin cooking by browning the meat in a non-stick pan over medium heat. As the beef cooks, it will release its flavorful juices, eliminating the need for additional oil or fat. This satisfying protein source is a favorite amongst our canine companions and a key contributor to their overall health. It supports

growth, muscle development, and cellular repair, making it a vital component in their diet.

2. As the enticing aroma of the cooking beef fills your kitchen, shift your attention to the vegetables. Butternut squash is the first on the chopping block with its subtly sweet flavor and vibrant orange hue. Follow it by dicing the crunchy carrots into small, bite-sized pieces. Both veggies are rich in vitamins and minerals that promote good health in dogs, including vitamin A for eye health and dietary fiber for digestion.

3. Once the ground beef is well-cooked and exudes a mouthwatering aroma, it's time to bring in the veggies. Add the diced butternut squash and carrots to the pan. Stir everything together, ensuring the vegetables are well-coated in the flavorful juices from the beef. This enhances the taste of the vegetables and makes the meal more enticing for your dog.

4. You can prepare the peas while the beef and veggies are simmering away. These little green gems are a great source of plant-based protein packed with several vitamins and minerals. If you're using frozen peas, thaw them under warm water. They'll need a quick boil until tender if you're using fresh peas.

5. Now, for the grand finale. Add the peas to the mix once the beef and veggies are fully cooked. Stir everything together, ensuring the ingredients are evenly distributed. The result is a medley of flavors and textures, creating a meal pleasing to the palate and loaded with nutrients.

6. Let it cool down before you present this culinary masterpiece to your furry friend. This is an important safety measure to prevent your dog from burning their mouth. The flavors will meld together as the meal cools, making it even more delicious.

Behold, the culmination - a simple, nutritious, and budget-friendly grain-free meal that can be whipped up quickly. This meal hits all the right notes. It's high in protein, packed with vitamins and minerals, and free from any grains that could upset your dog's stomach. And the best part? It's made with love, from your kitchen to your dog's bowl. So, the next time you're looking for a quick, grain-free meal for your pup, give this recipe a go. It might just become their new favorite!

Fish and Green Beans Grain-Free Recipe

When maintaining your fur baby's health, feeding them a balanced diet is a significant factor. And if your pup has a sensitive tummy, this grain-free recipe might be the answer. Let's check out another palate-pleasing, grain-free recipe with fresh salmon fillets, sweet potatoes, and green beans, all with a drizzle of olive oil. Not only is this meal a feast for your dog's taste buds, but it's also a nutritional powerhouse. Ready to get your paws dirty in the kitchen? Let's dig in!

Serving Size:

- For small breeds (½ to 1 cup per meal), the recipe could provide around 6 to 12 servings.
- For medium breeds (1 to 2.5 cups per meal), it would yield approximately 2.5 to 6 servings.
- For large breeds (2.5 to 4 cups per meal), it might yield about 1.5 to 3 servings.

Ingredients:

- 1 pound fresh salmon fillets
- 1 cups green beans
- 2 cups sweet potatoes
- 1 tablespoon olive oil

Recipe Time:

1. Our recipe begins with the star of the show, fresh salmon fillets. Salmon is a lean protein and omega-3 fatty acids, vital for maintaining your dog's skin and coat health. To start, sear the salmon fillets in a non-stick pan over medium heat. You won't need any oil since salmon naturally contains oils that will release as it cooks. Ensure the fillets are cooked until they're opaque and flake easily with a fork.

2. As the salmon cooks, you can turn your attention to the vegetables. Begin with the sweet potatoes. Peel and dice them into bite-sized pieces. Sweet potatoes contain dietary fiber and essential nutrients like vitamin A. Next, move on to the green beans. Rinse them and chop them into bite-sized pieces. These vibrant veggies add color to the dish and provide healthy vitamins and minerals.

3. You can start cooking the vegetables once the salmon is fully cooked and set aside to cool. Add the diced sweet potatoes to a pot of boiling water and let them simmer until tender. This process should take about 10-15 minutes. Put the green beans in the pot for the last five minutes of cooking. This will ensure the sweet potatoes and green beans are perfectly cooked – soft enough for your dog to chew and digest quickly.

4. Now, back to the salmon. Once it has cooled sufficiently, you can flake it into small, bite-sized pieces. Be vigilant during this step, and make sure to remove any tiny bones that might be lurking within the fillets.

5. Once all your ingredients are prepared, it's time to assemble the meal. Combine the flaked salmon, cooked sweet potatoes, and chopped green beans in a large bowl. Stir everything together until well mixed. To finish, drizzle a tablespoon of olive oil over the mixture. Olive oil contributes to a shiny coat and healthier skin for your dog because it contains healthy fats.

Lo and behold! A grain-free, nutritionally balanced meal that's quick to prepare and packed with the nutrients your dog needs. Plus, it's sure to get your dog's tail wagging in delight! The salmon provides lean protein and beneficial omega-3 fatty acids, the sweet potatoes offer a great source of fiber and vitamins, and the green beans add color and a boost of vitamins.

Feeding your dog a grain-free diet doesn't mean you have to compromise on taste or nutrition. With recipes like this, you can provide your fur baby with the wholesome, homemade meals they deserve while catering to their dietary needs. So, the next time you're planning your dog's meals, remember this recipe. It's quick, easy, and sure to get your dog excited at mealtime.

Turkey and Carrots Grain-Free Feast

There's something about a good feast that brings joy to the heart, whether you walk on two legs or four. And when it comes to our dogs, we want to offer feasts that aren't just tasty but also loaded with the nutrients they need. So, here's a grain-free feast featuring ground turkey, carrots, peas, and zucchini to get your dog's tail wagging!

Serving Size:

- For small breeds (½ to 1 cup per meal), the recipe could provide around 6 to 12 servings.
- For medium breeds (1 to 2.5 cups per meal), it would yield approximately 2.5 to 6 servings.
- For large breeds (2.5 to 4 cups per meal), it might yield about 1.5 to 3 servings.

Ingredients:

- 1 pound ground turkey
- 1 cup carrots
- 1 cup peas
- 1 cup zucchini

Recipe Time:

1. Ground turkey takes center stage in this recipe. Begin by browning the turkey in a non-stick pan over medium heat until it's fully cooked. As the turkey cooks, it will release its own juices, eliminating the need for additional oil. Ground turkey is a lean protein source, essential for maintaining your dog's muscles and supporting their overall body function.
2. While the turkey is cooking, you can focus on the veggies. Please start with the carrots, peeling and dicing them into small, bite-sized pieces. Move on to the zucchini, following the same process. Lastly, if you're using fresh peas, rinse them under cold water. These veggies add a burst of color to the meal and provide a variety of vitamins and minerals.
3. Once the turkey is fully cooked, it's time to add the veggies. Start by adding the diced carrots and zucchini to the pan. Stir everything to ensure the veggies are well-coated in the turkey's flavorful juices. Next, add the peas and cook over medium heat until the vegetables are tender. This should take about 10-15 minutes.
4. Once everything is cooked and the flavors have melded together, allow the meal to cool before serving it to your dog. This ensures your dog can enjoy its meal without the risk of burning its mouth.

Eureka, we've arrived – a hearty, grain-free feast that's as nutritious as delicious. The ground turkey provides lean protein, the carrots, and zucchini are a great source of fiber and essential vitamins, and the peas add some color and boost vitamins.

Feeding your dog a grain-free diet doesn't mean you have to compromise on variety or flavor. With the right ingredients and a sprinkle of creativity, you can whip up meals that cater to your dog's dietary needs, tantalize their taste buds, and contribute to their overall health.

So, the next time you plan your dog's meal, try this recipe. It's quick, easy, and sure to make mealtime a feast to remember.

With every recipe you try, you're feeding your dog and taking an active role in their health and well-being. You're showing them love in the most tangible way possible – through delicious, nutritious meals prepared with care.

As we move forward, we'll continue exploring the wonderful world of homemade dog food, jumping into treats and snacks to help you navigate this exciting culinary landscape. So, keep those pots ready, those tails wagging, and turn the page!

German Shorthaired Pointers are the Olympic athletes of the dog world, with endless energy and the focus of a laser beam on anything that moves. They're like four-legged, tail-wagging GPS systems, always on the move, mapping out the best routes through fields, forests, and occasionally your living room.

8

TANTALIZING TREATS AND SNACKS: SPOILING YOUR POOCH THE HEALTHY WAY

S ometimes, love comes in the form of a belly rub or a game of fetch. Other times, a homemade biscuit, still warm from the oven, gets your dog's tail wagging. Welcome to the delightful realm of homemade dog treats and snacks. Here, we trade the preservative-laden store-bought biscuits for wholesome, budget-friendly, and drool-worthy homemade alternatives. Ready to whip up some tail-wagging goodness for your four-legged friend? Let's get baking!

Peanut Butter and Banana Dog Biscuits: A Tail-Wagging Delight

Think of being cuddled up on the couch with your furry best friend, watching your favorite movie. Your hand reaches for a bowl of popcorn, and those adorable, pleading eyes turn your way. We've all been there. Imagine if you could offer a dog-friendly treat at that moment. A treat that's not only tasty but also made with simple, nutritious ingredients. Sounds perfect. Let's make it happen with this Peanut Butter and Banana Dog Biscuits recipe.

Serving Size:

- For small breeds, the recipe would yield about 24 to 36 servings.
- For medium breeds, it would yield approximately 12 to 36 servings.
- For large breeds, it might yield about 8 to 18 servings.

Ingredients:

- 2 cups whole wheat flour
- 1 cup oats
- 1 cup peanut butter
- 2 ripe bananas

Recipe Time:

1. Start by preheating the oven: This initial step is crucial for baking. Set your oven to 350°F (175°C) and prepare a baking sheet with parchment paper. This prevents the biscuits from sticking to the sheet and makes cleanup a breeze.
2. Combine the dry components: Use a large bowl to mix 2 cups of whole wheat flour and 1 cup of oats, forming the foundation of our biscuits. Whole wheat flour provides a substantial amount of fiber. At the same time, oats are rich in essential vitamins and minerals beneficial for your dog's well-being.
3. Add wet ingredients: Mash 2 ripe bananas in a different bowl and blend in 1 cup of peanut butter. Bananas offer an abundance of vitamins and minerals, and peanut butter, rich in protein, is typically a favorite among dogs.
4. Combine everything: Add the banana and peanut butter mixture to the bowl with the flour and oats. Stir everything together until you have a dough that's easy to handle. If the dough is too sticky, you can add a bit more flour.
5. Form the biscuits: This is where the enjoyment begins! Roll the dough on a surface dusted with flour and use a cookie

cutter to shape the biscuits. Feel free to choose any design you prefer – bones, hearts, or your dog's initials. Ensure the biscuits are sized appropriately for your dog to safely consume.

6. Bake the biscuits: Place them on your prepared baking sheet for about 15-20 minutes until golden brown and crispy. Baking time can vary depending on the size of the biscuits, so keep an eye on them to prevent burning.

7. Cool and serve: Once the biscuits are done, let them cool before giving them to your dog. This is essential as it prevents your dog from burning its mouth and gives the biscuits time to become nice and crunchy.

And ta-da: a delicious, homemade treat that will set your dog's tail a-wagging! These biscuits are not only a healthier alternative to store-bought treats, but they're also a wonderful way to show your dog some love. They're great for special occasions, training rewards, or just because.

While treats are a fun addition to your dog's diet, they should not make up more than 10% of their daily calorie intake. Constantly adjust meal portions accordingly and consult your vet if you have any questions about your dog's nutritional needs.

So, the next time you're curled up on the couch with your furry friend, reach for these homemade biscuits instead of that bowl of popcorn. Your dog will thank you for it, and you'll feel good knowing you're giving them a treat that's tasty and good for them. Now, that's what I call a win-win!

So, keep that apron on, those oven mitts handy, and your dog's taste buds ready for more homemade treats and snacks. Trust me, with recipes like these, you'll have your dog doing tricks they didn't even know they could do!

Chicken and Apple Doggie Treats: A Healthy Indulgence

Gone are the days when dog treats were dry, bone-shaped biscuits that tasted like cardboard. Our furry friends deserve better, don't they? So, let's step up our treat game with a recipe that combines lean chicken breast, juicy apples, whole wheat flour, and eggs. These ingredients come together to create a treat that's not only delicious but also nutritious. So, tie on that apron, preheat your oven, and start baking!

Serving Size:

- For small breeds, the recipe would yield about 24 to 36 servings.
- For medium breeds, it would yield approximately 12 to 36 servings.
- For large breeds, it might yield about 8 to 18 servings.

Ingredients:

- 1 chicken breast
- 1 large apple
- 2 cups whole wheat flour
- 2 eggs

Recipe Time:

1. Our first step is to cook the chicken breast. Chicken is a lean protein that supports muscle growth and repair. Place the chicken breast in boiling water and let it simmer until fully cooked. This should take about 15-20 minutes depending on the breast size. Once it's done, remove it from the pot and let it cool.
2. While the chicken is cooling, you can get started on the apples. Apples are a great source of fiber and vitamins A and

C. Plus, their natural sweetness makes them a hit with most dogs. Wash, core, and grate one large apple. No need to peel the apple as the skin has additional nutrients.

3. Now comes the fun part! After the chicken is cooled, you can shred it into bite-sized pieces. Transfer the shredded chicken to a large bowl, add the grated apple, 2 cups of whole wheat flour, and 2 eggs. The whole wheat flour gives the treat structure, while the eggs act as a binding agent.

4. Mix everything until you have a firm dough. If the dough is too sticky, you can add a bit more flour. Roll out the dough on a floured surface and cut out shapes using a cookie cutter. You can get creative here - use different shapes or sizes based on your dog's size and preference.

5. Arrange the cutouts on a baking sheet lined with parchment paper. Bake them in the oven at 350°F (175°C) for around 20-25 minutes or until golden brown and crispy.

6. Once the treats are ready, remove them from the oven and let them cool. This makes the treats crunchier and ensures your dog won't burn their mouth.

Great job! You've created a batch of chicken and apple doggie treats that will make your fur baby's tail wag with delight. These treats are a tasty indulgence for your dog and a healthy one. The chicken provides lean protein, the apple adds sweetness and fiber, and the whole wheat flour and eggs hold everything together.

So, the next time you want to reward your pup for being the good boy or girl they are, reach for these homemade treats. They're a testament to the fact that treats can be tasty and healthy. Plus, they're made with love, which, as we all know, is the most essential ingredient of all.

In the journey of homemade dog food, treats like these are the scenic stops that make the ride even more enjoyable. They're the little indulgences that bring joy to your dog's day and a smile to your face. Because, at the end of the day, it's about more than just feeding your dog. It's about nourishing them with quality ingredients, supporting their health, and showing them just how much they're loved. So, let's continue this incredible journey, one treat at a time.

Sweet Potato Dog Chews: A Chewy Delight

Did you know that sweet potatoes are a powerhouse of nutrition? Packed with fiber, vitamins, and antioxidants, they're a fantastic addition to your dog's diet. But wait, there's more! They also make great chews that your dog will love. So, how about we whip up some sweet potato dog chews? They're easy to make, budget-friendly, and guaranteed to get that tail wagging!

Serving Size:

- For small breeds, the recipe would yield about 24 servings.
- For medium breeds, it would yield approximately 12 to 24 servings.
- For large breeds, it might yield about 8 to 12 servings.

Ingredients:

- 2 large sweet potatoes
- sprinkle cinnamon
- pour melted coconut oil

Recipe Time:

1. Start with washing and peeling the sweet potatoes. The next step is to slice them, but hold on a second. The thicker the slices, the chewy they will be. If your dog enjoys a good gnaw, slice them half an inch thick. For a softer chew, go for a quarter of an inch. Always cut the slices lengthwise to make

them longer, providing a satisfying chew for your furry friend.

2. Next, let's add a little pizzazz to our chews. Put the slices on a baking sheet and lightly dust them with cinnamon. Cinnamon adds a lovely aroma and flavor that dogs love and is rich in antioxidants that can help reduce inflammation. However, remember to use it sparingly, as too much can be overpowering for your pup's sensitive nose.

3. Now comes the secret ingredient - coconut oil. Sprinkle a small amount of melted coconut oil over the sweet potato slices. Coconut oil contains healthy fats and can help enhance skin and coat health. Plus, its subtle flavor complements the potatoes' sweetness and the cinnamon's warmth.

4. This is where patience comes in. The key to making chewy chews is slow cooking at a low temperature. Bake the sweet potato slices in a preheated oven at 250°F (120°C) for 2-3 hours. Halfway through, flip the slices to ensure they cook evenly. This slow cooking dehydrates the slices, giving them a chewy texture that dogs love.

5. Once the chews are done, let them cool completely. This makes them safer for your dog to eat and allows them to harden a bit more, enhancing their chewiness.

There they are - homemade sweet potato dog chews! They're a tasty, healthy, and cost-effective alternative to store-bought chews. Plus, they're made with love, which makes them even more special.

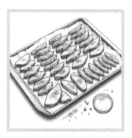

So, reach for these chews when your dog wants something to chew on or deserves a little treat. You'll satisfy your dog's chewing instinct and provide them with a nutritious treat. Plus, you'll enjoy seeing your dog happily gnawing on a chew you made. Now, that's a real treat!

Remember, while these chews are a great addition to your dog's diet, they are a treat and should be given in moderation. Always supervise your dog while enjoying a chew to ensure they don't accidentally swallow large pieces.

Keep your apron and oven mitts handy because we're still going! Stay tuned for more delicious, nutritious, and budget-friendly homemade dog treats and snacks. Each recipe satisfies your dog's taste buds and nourishes their body with wholesome ingredients. And that, dear reader, is the true joy of homemade dog food.

Pumpkin and Oat Dog Cookies: A Crunchy Delight

Ready to add another irresistible recipe to your homemade dog treat repertoire? We will blend the natural sweetness of pumpkin with the hearty goodness of oats, a hint of cinnamon, and the structural support of whole wheat flour. The end result? Crunchy, nutritious cookies that will have your dog doing a happy dance at treat time. So, let's roll up our sleeves and get started!

Serving Size:

- For small breeds, the recipe would yield about 24 to 36 servings.
- For medium breeds, it would yield approximately 12 to 36 servings.
- For large breeds, it might yield about 8 to 18 servings.

Ingredients:

- 1 cup pumpkin puree
- 2 cups oats
- 1 ½ cups whole wheat flour
- sprinkle of cinnamon

Recipe Time:

1. Our recipe starts with pumpkin puree, a nutrient-rich ingredient with a sweet and smooth texture. Pumpkin is a source of fiber, which helps support your dog's digestive health. It's also packed with essential vitamins and minerals, making it a wholesome addition to your dog's diet. You'll need about a cup of pumpkin puree for this recipe, which you can either buy pre-made or make at home by cooking and pureeing a fresh pumpkin.

2. Next, we'll add oats to the mix, precisely rolled oats. Oats are a fantastic source of slow-releasing energy packed with dietary fiber. They also contribute to the texture of the cookies, giving them a delightful crunch that dogs love. For this recipe, you'll need about two cups of rolled oats.

3. The next ingredient on our list is whole wheat flour. This type of flour is made from whole grains, meaning it retains all its natural nutrients, including dietary fiber, protein, and various essential minerals. In our recipe, the wheat flour serves as the binding agent, helping to hold the cookies together as they bake. This recipe requires about a cup and a half of whole wheat flour.

4. Lastly, we'll add a sprinkle of cinnamon. This warm, fragrant spice enhances the flavors of the pumpkin and oats, adding a depth of flavor that makes these cookies irresistible. Cinnamon has anti-inflammatory properties, making it a great addition to your dog's diet. Just remember to use it sparingly—a little goes a long way!

5. It's time to create the cookie dough with all your ingredients ready. Combine the pumpkin puree, oats, whole wheat flour, and a sprinkle of cinnamon in a large bowl. Stir everything together until well mixed. The resulting dough should be firm yet pliable, easy to roll out, and cut into shapes.

6. Roll the dough out on a floured surface, making it a quarter of an inch thick. Using a cookie cutter of your choice, cut out the cookies and place them on a baking sheet lined with parchment paper.

7. Bake the cookies in an oven at 350°F (175°C) for approximately 25-30 minutes until golden brown and crispy. The baking time can vary depending on the size of your cookies, so keep a close eye on them to prevent burning.

8. Once they are done, take the cookies from the oven and let them cool completely. This makes them crunchier and ensures they're safe for your dog to eat.

Just like magic, there it is—a batch of homemade pumpkin and oat dog cookies that are as nutritious as they are delicious. These cookies make an excellent treat for training, rewarding, or simply showing your dog some love. Plus, they're made with simple, wholesome ingredients you can feel good about.

So, the next time your dog gives you those puppy dog eyes, reach for these homemade treats. They're sure to be a hit with their satisfying crunch and delicious flavor. Plus, you'll know what's in them, which is more than can be said for most store-bought treats.

Remember, these treats are intended to supplement your dog's diet and should make up no more than 10% of their daily calorie intake. Also, it's always a good idea to consult your vet before implementing new foods into your dog's diet.

Our next chapter is on meal prepping. You'll learn how to be ready and prepared to whip up these delicious homemade meals for your pup. Learning to prep your dog's meals will help you to create meals and treats that cater to your dog's dietary needs and taste preferences with a dash of creativity and a sprinkle of love. And that, dear reader, is the joy of homemade dog food.

Pembroke Welsh Corgis are the royal jesters of the dog kingdom, with their short legs orchestrating a waddle that could disarm even the sternest of hearts. They're like loaves of bread with legs, blessed with a bark that commands more authority than their stature suggests, proving that good things come in small, fluffy packages.

9

MEAL PREPPING 101: MAKING HOMEMADE DOG FOOD EASIER

It's Sunday afternoon, the kitchen is alive with the aroma of simmering stews, and the oven is working its magic on a fresh batch of dog-friendly biscuits. Your furry friend is wagging their tail in anticipation, their nose twitching at the delicious smells wafting through the air. On the countertop, you have a week's worth of nutritious, homemade dog meals ready to be portioned and stored. Welcome to the world of meal prepping for dogs. It's about making homemade dog food more manageable, efficient, and enjoyable.

Meal prepping is like having your cake and eating it too, except in this case, the cake is a well-nourished pup, and eating is your dog's delight at mealtime. It's about dedicating a few hours each week to plan, shop, and cook and then reap the rewards for days to come. It's a game-changer, a stress reliever, and a time-saver all rolled into one. Ready to give it a try? Let's do this!

The Basics of Meal Prepping for Dogs

Planning a Weekly Menu: The Blueprint to Success

Planning is vital to successful meal prepping. It's like setting out on a road trip with a well-planned route, ensuring you reach your destination without any hiccups.

Start by deciding how many meals you want to prep. Are you planning to go all in and prepare your dog's meals for the week? You may want to ease into it and only prep a few days' worth. Whatever your goal, having a clear idea of how many meals you need to prepare will set the foundation for your meal-prepping plan.

Next, choose the recipes you want to make. Variety is essential for your dog's nutritional needs and to keep them interested in their food. Consider rotating between two to three recipes to provide a mix of different proteins, grains, and vegetables.

Shopping for Ingredients: The Prepping Prequel

Once you have your weekly menu, list all the ingredients you need. Arrange your list based on the sections of the grocery store. This will save you time and ensure you remember everything.

When shopping for ingredients, consider buying in bulk. This is often more cost-effective and ensures you have enough ingredients for all your meals. Remember to check the expiration dates, especially for fresh produce and meats, to ensure they will last until you are ready to cook them.

Organizing Your Kitchen for Efficiency: Every Tool in its Place

An organized kitchen is a meal prepper's best friend. Knowing where everything is saves time and makes the cooking process smoother.

Start by ensuring all your kitchen tools and appliances are clean and ready to use. There's nothing worse than reaching for a pot or a chopping board and realizing it's dirty.

Next, organize your ingredients. Group them based on the recipes they belong to. This way, when you're ready to start cooking, everything you need is in one place.

Now, with your menu planned, ingredients purchased, and kitchen organized, you're ready to start meal prepping. It's time to bring out the apron, put on some music, and embrace the joy of cooking for your furry friend. As the pots start simmering and the oven begins its magic, take a moment to appreciate the journey you're on. You're preparing meals and investing in your dog's health and happiness, one meal at a time.

And who knows? You might find that meal prepping isn't a chore but a labor of love, a weekly ritual that brings you as much joy as it does your eagerly waiting pup.

Safe Storage Practices for Homemade Dog Food: Keeping it Fresh and Tasty

Proper Cooling Before Storage: The Chill Factor

Let's begin with the cooling process. Once your culinary creations are ready, they must cool down before storing them. This crucial step helps prevent the growth of bacteria, which can spoil the food and potentially harm your furry friend. So, how do you cool the food properly? It's simple. After cooking, take the food from the heat source and allow it to sit at room temperature. But remember, you don't want to leave it out sitting too long. Ideally, the food should cool down within two hours.

Using Airtight Containers: Seal in the Goodness

Next up, let's talk about containers. The correct storage containers can make a difference in preserving the quality of your homemade dog food. You'll want to opt for airtight containers, champions for keeping food fresh and tasty. They create a seal that locks out air, preventing it from reaching the food. This helps keep the food moist, retains the flavors, and slows spoiling.

When choosing containers, consider the size. You'll want containers that can comfortably hold the portion sizes you'll be serving. This way, you can grab a container from the fridge or freezer during meal-time without worrying about measuring portions.

Labeling and Dating Stored Food: Mark Their Calendars

This may seem like a small step, but it can make a big difference, especially if you're making large batches of food. Clearly labeling each container with the contents and the date it was created can save you from playing the guessing game later on. Plus, it helps ensure you're feeding your dog the oldest meals first, so nothing goes to waste.

The date on the label also serves as a reminder of how long the food has been stored. Generally, homemade dog food can be stored in the refrigerator for three to five days. If you're still determining if your dog will consume all the food within that timeframe, it's best to freeze the excess.

In the freezer, homemade dog food can last around two to three months. With the food neatly packaged in portion-sized, clearly labeled containers, you'll have a ready supply of meals at your fingertips.

And so the pieces fall into place, a simple and efficient system for safely storing your homemade dog food. With these steps, you can ensure that each meal you've carefully prepared retains its quality, flavor, and nutritional value, from your kitchen to your dog's bowl. After all, your dog deserves nothing but the best, and that includes enjoying their meals as fresh and tasty as they were the moment you made them.

Preparing Large Batches: A Week's Worth of Meals

Doubling or Tripling Recipes: More of the Good Stuff

Ever tried a new recipe and wished you had made more? Making more is often a wise move when it comes to homemade dog food. Doubling or tripling a recipe means you spend the same time cooking but have multiple meals. This is especially handy for recipes your dog particularly enjoys.

To double or triple a recipe, multiply each ingredient by two or three. For example, doubling a recipe for 1 cup of chicken and 2 carrots would require 2 cups of chicken and 4 carrots. It's as simple as that. Just bear in mind that cooking times may vary slightly with larger quantities.

Using Slow Cookers for Bulk Cooking: The Set-and-Forget Method

If you're a fan of hands-off cooking, then you'll love using a slow cooker for meal prep. These magical machines do the hard work for you, slowly simmering your ingredients to perfection while you go about your day. Plus, they're perfect for bulk cooking.

You'll need recipes specifically designed for slow cooking to use a slow cooker, or you can adapt your favorite recipes. Add enough liquid to prevent the food from drying out, but not so much that it ends up soupy.

Fill your slow cooker with your ingredients, set it low, and let it work magic. Most recipes need 6-8 hours on low or 3-4 hours on high. Once cooked, allow the food to cool before portioning and storing.

Dividing Meals into Daily Portions: Mealtime Made Easy

Once you've cooked your large batch of food, the next step is dividing it into daily portions. This makes mealtime a breeze and ensures your dog gets the right amount of food each day.

To do this, you'll need to know how much food your dog needs daily. This depends on your dog's size, age, activity level, and any specific dietary requirements. If you need more clarification, your vet can provide guidance.

Once you know your dog's daily food requirement, you can start portioning. Use a measuring cup to ensure accuracy. Scoop the appropriate amount of food into your storage containers, then seal and store as required.

With your meals portioned and ready to go, feeding your dog becomes as simple as grabbing a container from the fridge or freezer. No more last-minute cooking or resorting to less healthy options because you need more time. Just nutritious, homemade food at your fingertips, ready to delight your dog at mealtime.

By preparing large batches of homemade dog food, you're making mealtime easier and ensuring your dog has a steady supply of nutritious, delicious meals. It's a way of showing your love for your furry friend, making your life a little easier. And when it comes to our dogs, anything that brings them happiness and keeps them healthy is worth every minute we spend on it.

The Freeze-Thaw-Reheat Trio: Maximizing Meal Longevity

Freezing Meals in Individual Portions: The Cold Storage Solution

Ever played a game of Tetris with your freezer? It's all fun and games until you can't find the meal you prepped last week. Storing meals in individual portions not only makes for more accessible organization but also ensures each meal stays fresh until it's time to serve.

To freeze your dog's meals, first ensure they're completely cooled. Then, choose freezer-safe containers that can comfortably hold one serving size. This strategy is a real time-saver; you can grab a container and go. No more scrambling to portion a meal while your dog does the "hungry dance" around your feet.

Thawing Frozen Meals Safely: Waking Up the Goodness

A frozen meal can be a lifesaver on a busy day. But it's essential to thaw it properly to maintain its quality and safety. A simple and safe way to thaw frozen dog food is in the refrigerator. This slow-thawing method minimizes the risk of bacterial growth, which can occur if food is left to thaw at room temperature.

Plan ahead and move a container from the freezer to the refrigerator the night before you need it. By mealtime the next day, it'll be safely and thoroughly thawed. Remember, once thawed, the meal should be used within 48 hours to ensure freshness.

Reheating Guidelines: Warming Up to Perfection

Some dogs are happy to eat their meals cold from the fridge. But if your pup prefers warm meals, there are a few things to remember.

Reheating should be done before and only for the portion you're about to serve. This is where those individual portions come in handy again! You can reheat the meal in the microwave, but remember to stir it thoroughly afterward to even out any hot spots.

Be sure to check the temperature of the meal before serving it to your dog. It should be warm to the touch, not hot. A good rule of thumb is to test it on your wrist, much like you would with baby formula. It'll be comfortable for your dog if it's comfortable for you.

When it comes to reheating, less is more. It's better to serve a slightly under-heated meal than risk burning your dog's mouth with too hot food. After all, the goal is to make mealtime enjoyable for your furry friend.

Thus, the puzzle is complete! These strategies and insights can help you master meal preparation, storage, and serving with expertise. Remember, the goal is to simplify making homemade dog food, ensuring efficiency and convenience without sacrificing the quality or nutritional value. So, here's to less stress, more time, and healthier, happier dogs.

In the next chapter, we'll explore another crucial aspect of home-made dog food: understanding and calculating portion sizes. So, keep those measuring cups ready! We're about to dive deep into portion control and its importance to your dog's health. Keep your eyes peeled!

Australian Shepherds are the multitasking maestros of the dog world, with a herding instinct so strong they might try to organize your house guests. They're like furry, four-legged whirlwinds of energy and intelligence, always ready for a challenge, whether catching frisbees or keeping an eye on the family cat.

10

THE RIGHT BITE: UNDERSTANDING AND CALCULATING YOUR DOG'S PORTION SIZES

W hen you're at a family barbecue, how do you decide how much to put on your plate? You may consider your hunger levels, the number of hours until your next meal, the tempting dessert awaiting, or even the number of calories you've burned during your morning workout. Essentially, you're calculating portion sizes based on your body's needs.

Now, let's switch gears and think about our furry friends. How do we decide how much to serve them for each meal? They can't tell us if they're still hungry or if they're feeling a tad too full. That's where portion control comes into play. Feeding your dog a balanced diet is necessary, ensuring they're getting just the right amount of food—no more, no less.

Determining Your Dog's Calorie Needs

Like humans, dogs have specific calorie needs based on various factors. Too few calories, and they could lose weight and lack energy. Too many, and they could pile on the pounds, leading to obesity-related health issues. So, how do we strike a balance? Here's a three-step process to help you determine your dog's calorie needs.

Assessing Your Dog's Activity Level

Think of your dog's lifestyle. If you have a Border Collie who herds sheep all day or a Labrador that can't resist a good game of fetch, they're likely burning many calories. On the other hand, if your Bulldog prefers a stroll around the block or your Pug spends most of the day snoozing, they probably need to use up more calories.

Just like an athlete needs more food than a desk worker, an active dog needs more calories than a less active one. So, the first step in determining your dog's calorie needs is to assess their activity level.

Factoring in Age and Health Status

Next, consider your dog's age and health status. Puppies grow rapidly and need more calories than adult dogs. Senior dogs may have slower metabolisms and require fewer calories. Pregnant or lactating dogs have higher energy needs, while neutered or spayed dogs may need fewer calories.

Health status also plays a role. Your dog's calorie needs may change if it is recovering from surgery or is sick. Some health conditions may require a special diet.

Consulting with Your Vet

The final and most crucial step is to consult with your vet. They know your dog's health history and can provide personalized advice based on your dog's needs.

They might recommend a special diet for a health condition or suggest a feeding plan for a puppy or pregnant dog. They can also help you understand the calorie content of different types of food, making it easier to calculate portion sizes.

Remember, every dog is different, and what works for one might not work for another. There's no one-size-fits-all when determining your dog's calorie needs. It's a delicate balance that requires observation, adjustment, and professional guidance. But the effort is well worth it. After all, nothing beats the satisfaction of knowing you're providing your dog with the nutrition they need to live their best life.

So, grab that notepad, observe your pup, and schedule a chat with your vet. You're about to crack the code on your dog's calorie needs. And with this knowledge, you'll be one step closer to mastering the art of portion control, serving up meals just right for your furry friend. The following section will go deeper into this topic and teach you how to calculate portion sizes based on these calorie needs. Get ready!

Calculating Portion Sizes: It's All in the Details

You've done the legwork—you've monitored your pup's activity levels, considered their age and health condition, and even chatted with your vet about their caloric needs. With this valuable information, it's time to roll up our sleeves and get into the nitty-gritty of portion sizes.

Understanding Caloric Content of Ingredients: A Nutritional Breakdown

Every ingredient in your dog's bowl carries a certain amount of calories. A chunk of beef, a scoop of brown rice, or a sprinkle of peas contribute to the meal's total caloric content. But how do you figure out the calories in each ingredient?

This is where nutrition labels or a quick online search can be helpful. Most packaged ingredients come with labels that list the calories per serving. Numerous online resources can provide the caloric content per ounce or cup for fresh produce or meats.

It's important to consider that cooking methods can alter the caloric content of certain foods. For instance, a raw carrot has fewer calories than a cooked one. Therefore, always look for the caloric content of the ingredient in the form you'll be using.

Adjusting Portions Based on Calorie Needs: The Balancing Act

Now that you know both your dog's daily caloric needs and the caloric content of each ingredient, you can start tailoring portion sizes. The goal is to meet your dog's caloric needs without going overboard.

Let's say your dog needs 800 calories daily, and you're planning two meals. That means each meal should be around 400 calories. If you're preparing a chicken and rice dish and find that one cup of cooked chicken is about 200 calories, and one cup of cooked rice is about 200 calories, you'd serve your dog one cup each for a meal.

However, remember to make your dog's meals balanced. You wouldn't want to feed your dog a meal that's all chicken or all rice just because it meets the caloric needs. Variety is vital to a balanced diet, so ensure each meal includes a protein source, carbohydrates, and vegetables.

Using Measuring Cups for Accuracy: Precision Is Key

Estimating portion sizes can be tricky, and accuracy is important when it comes to feeding your dog. Providing the correct portion is where measuring cups become your best friend. They can help you accurately portion each ingredient to ensure your dog gets the necessary amount of food.

When using measuring cups, level off the cup for dry ingredients and read liquid measurements at eye level. Consistency is critical, so try using the same measuring cup set each time.

Remember, each dog is different, and their nutritional needs can change over time. Regular check-ins with your vet and close observation of your dog's weight, body condition, and overall health are crucial.

Portion control in dogs is more than just a way to prevent weight gain —it's a fundamental part of a balanced diet. It ensures your dog gets the right amount of food and the necessary nutrients to stay healthy and thrive. With these tips and some practice, you'll be a pro at portion control, serving up just the right amount of food for your furry friend.

So, grab that measuring cup and start portioning. Your dog's balanced, perfectly portioned meals are just a scoop away!

The next section will look at adjusting portions for weight loss or gain. Modifying portions is essential for maintaining your dog's healthy weight, so be sure to check it out.

Adjusting Portions for Weight Loss or Gain: The Scale Balancing Act

Like humans, maintaining a healthy weight in our furry friends is vital for their health and longevity. It's a delicate balance that requires careful monitoring and occasional adjustments. Whether your canine companion needs to shed a few pounds or bulk up, understanding how to adjust their meal portions is crucial.

Reducing Portions for Weight Loss: The Calorie Cutback

If your vet has given your dog the side-eye during their last check-up or your pup is panting after a short walk, consider a weight loss plan. The first step? Reducing portion sizes.

Start by revisiting your dog's current daily calorie intake. If your dog has been maintaining weight on this diet, reducing intake by about 10% is a safe starting point for weight loss.

However, nutrition is still necessary. Your dog still needs a balanced diet. You can achieve this by slightly reducing the amount of each ingredient in your dog's meal. For example, if your dog's meal typically includes a cup of chicken, half a cup of brown rice, and a cup of mixed vegetables, you could reduce this to three-quarters of a cup of chicken, less than half a cup of rice, and three-quarters of a cup of vegetables.

Remember, weight loss should be gradual to be safe and sustainable. A sudden decrease in food can leave your dog hungry and lead to nutrient deficiencies.

Increasing Portions for Weight Gain: More is More

On the other end of the scale, if your dog has been looking a little too lean or your vet has suggested they could benefit from gaining a few pounds, it's time to up those portion sizes.

Begin by increasing their daily calorie intake by about 10%. You can increase calorie intake by adding more of each meal ingredient. If your dog's standard meal includes a cup of beef, half a cup of quinoa, and a cup of carrots, you could increase this to a cup and a quarter of beef, slightly more than half a cup of quinoa, and a cup and a quarter of carrots.

Just like with weight loss, weight gain should be gradual. An abrupt increase in food could lead to digestive upset or rapid weight gain, which could have health implications.

Monitoring Weight Changes: The Weigh-In

Regular weight checks are necessary whether you're adjusting portions for weight loss or gain. Weigh your dog every week to monitor progress. Remember, weight changes should be gradual—around 1-2% of their weight per week.

But rely on more than just the scale. Take note of your dog's body condition, too. Can you feel (but not see) your dog's ribs? Are they energetic and eager to play? These signs can help you assess whether their diet is on the right track.

Finally, keep in touch with your vet. They can provide guidance and support throughout the process and help you make necessary adjustments to your dog's diet.

Adjusting portions for weight loss or gain is not a one-time task. It's a continuous part of caring for your dog, ensuring they stay in tip-top shape. With careful monitoring, periodic check-ins with your vet, and a good understanding of portion sizes, you can help your dog reach and keep a healthy weight. So, keep the scales handy, your vet on speed dial, and your measuring cups ready. A healthier, happier dog is well worth the effort.

Reading Your Dog's Hunger Signals: The Canine Communication Code

There's no Google Translate for 'dog'—yet. But that doesn't mean we can't understand what our furry pals are telling us. Dogs are pretty articulate when expressing their needs, particularly their hunger. So, let's decode these cues together and become pros at understanding our dogs' hunger signals.

Recognizing Signs of Hunger: The Telltale Signs

Dogs have unique ways of saying, "Hey, I'm hungry!" But certain universal signs can alert you to your dog's hunger.

The first sign is obvious—your dog shows interest in food. This could be your dog following you into the kitchen, sniffing around the food bowl, or even trying to snatch a morsel off your plate. Your pup might also become more energetic or excited around meal times, tail wagging and jumping in anticipation.

Another sign is a behavior change. Is your usually calm dog suddenly acting restless or anxious? Are they pacing around, whining, or pawing at you? These could all be indications that your dog's stomach is rumbling.

Lastly, pay attention to your dog's eating habits. Suppose your dog finishes their meals more quickly than usual or immediately looks for more once their bowl is empty. In that case, it might be a sign that they're not getting enough to eat.

Differentiating Between Hunger and Boredom: The Impostor Syndrome

Just like humans, dogs can sometimes mistake boredom for hunger. A bored dog might show many of the same signals as a hungry dog—pacing, whining, showing interest in food. So, how do you tell the difference?

A key factor is timing. If your dog ate its meal not too long ago and is now showing signs of hunger, they may be just bored. Another clue is their interest in play. A bored dog will usually be just as interested in a game of fetch as they are in a treat.

Also, consider your dog's overall behavior. Suppose your pup shows signs of hunger but is also destructive, excessively licking or chewing, or showing other signs of anxiety. In that case, they might be bored rather than hungry.

Responding to Changes in Appetite: The Action Plan

So, you've noticed a change in your dog's appetite. Now what? The answer depends on the change.

If your dog shows signs of hunger after finishing their meal, consider whether their portion size is correct. Are they getting enough food based on size, activity level, and life stage? If you need more clarification, consult with your vet.

If your dog is eating less than usual, consider whether there could be a medical reason. Is your pooch showing any signs of illness, such as lethargy, vomiting, or changes in stool? If so, it's time for a vet visit.

If you suspect your dog is eating out of boredom rather than hunger, it might be time to spice up their routine. Exercise, mental stimulation, and social interaction can all help keep boredom at bay.

And that's the gist. The art of understanding your dog's hunger signals is really about understanding your dog—knowing their habits, recognizing changes, and responding accordingly. It's another way to ensure our furry friends are happy, healthy, and living their best lives.

Remember, you know your dog better than anyone else. Trust your instincts, seek advice when needed, and keep doing what you're doing—loving and caring for your four-legged friend. Because that's what it's all about.

As we move forward, we'll continue to explore the fascinating world of homemade dog food, delving into more practical tips and expert advice to help you navigate this rewarding endeavor. So hang tight for more, keep those questions coming, and remember—you're doing a fantastic job. After all, cooking for your dog isn't just about feeding them; it's about nourishing them, body and soul. Here's to good food, happy dogs, and the humans who love them.

Yorkshire Terriers are the pint-sized powerhouses of the canine community, proving that great things come in small packages and a hefty dose of sass. They're like tiny, four-legged divas with the heart of a lion, ready to take on the world or a leaf blowing in the wind, all while maintaining their impeccable hairstyles.

11

SQUEEZING THE CLOCK: MAKING HOMEMADE DOG FOOD IN A TIME CRUNCH

It's a Tuesday evening. Work was a whirlwind, and you can still feel the echoes of a thousand tasks buzzing in your brain. You look at your dog, their eyes full of anticipation for their dinner. Pulling out pots and pans, chopping ingredients, and standing over the stove feels like a marathon you must prepare to run. But then you remember your dog's excited tail wag when they see their homemade meal, how they gobble it up enthusiastically, and the contented sigh it lets out when done. You know it's worth it, but how do you wish you had more time?

Well, my fellow dog devotees, I have good news. Homemade dog food doesn't have to be a time-consuming chore. With a few innovative strategies and a pinch of planning, you can whip up nutritious meals for your pooch without feeling like you're racing against the clock. Intrigued? Let's take a closer look.

Overcoming Time Constraints: Every Minute Counts

Utilizing Time-Saving Kitchen Tools: Your Culinary Comrades

Think about a painter. Would they attempt to paint a masterpiece without brushes? Or a writer trying to pen a novel without a keyboard? Tools in any craft can make the process more efficient and enjoyable. The same applies to cooking.

Take a moment to consider your kitchen. Do you have a slow cooker in a cupboard, gathering dust? Or a food processor used just a handful of times. These tools can be real time-savers when preparing homemade dog food.

A slow cooker, for instance, can be a game-changer. It lets you throw in your ingredients, set the timer, and go about your day. Hours later, you return to a fully cooked meal, ready to be served. It's like having a personal chef cooking for you while you're out and about.

A food processor, on the other hand, can drastically cut down your prep time. Chopping vegetables or grinding meat can be done in a matter of seconds. It's like having your sous chef handle the tedious tasks.

So, dust off those kitchen tools and put them to good use. They're not just space-fillers in your kitchen but your allies in the quest for time-efficient homemade dog food.

Incorporating Meal Prep into Your Routine: The Power of Planning

Have you ever noticed how we're likelier to stick to habits woven into our routines? Whether it's a morning jog or an evening meditation, when something becomes a part of our routine, it feels less like a task and more like a natural part of our day. The same principle applies to meal prepping.

Consider designating a specific day of the week as your "meal prep day." It could be a lazy Sunday afternoon or a mid-week Wednesday evening. On this day, you'll prepare your dog's meals for the entire week.

Start by picking out the recipes you want to prepare, listing the ingredients you need, and ensuring you have them all on hand. Then, get cooking. You might have multiple pots on the stove and perhaps something roasting in the oven. It might appear chaotic, but this couple of hours spent in the kitchen can save you countless more during the week.

After cooking all the meals, divide them into separate containers and place them in the refrigerator or freezer. Just like that, you've prepared a week's worth of meals. Remember, the goal isn't to create more work for yourself; it's to make feeding your dog homemade meals more manageable and less time-consuming.

Making the Most of Leftovers: Waste Not, Want Not

In the hustle and bustle of daily life, convenience is critical. And what could be more convenient than making use of leftovers? It's a win-win situation—you reduce waste and save time on meal prep.

Of course, ensuring any leftovers you intend to use are safe and healthy for your dog is crucial. Store foods appropriately and dispose of items that have surpassed their freshness. Remember, not all human foods are healthy for dogs. Ensure you avoid toxic ingredients to dogs, like chocolate, onions, or certain artificial sweeteners.

You can innovatively include leftovers in your dog's diet. Mix leftover vegetables into a meat dish, shred leftover chicken for a grain-based meal, and so forth. Variety is critical for a balanced diet, so utilizing leftovers provides your dog with diverse foods.

Ultimately, it's all about seamlessly making homemade dog food fit into your life. It's about finding ways to make the process more efficient so you can provide your dog with nutritious, homemade meals without feeling overwhelmed or pressed for time. Because at the end of the day, the time you spend preparing your dog's food is a testament to your love and care for them. And every wag of their tail, every contented sigh as they gobble up their meal, makes it all worthwhile.

Making Economically Smart Choices: Your Wallet's Best Friend

Buying Ingredients in Bulk: The Power of More for Less

Think about your go-to homemade dog food ingredients. Chicken? Carrots? Rice? Imagine having a bountiful supply of these staples at your fingertips, ready to be transformed into nutritious meals for your furry friend. Does this sound convenient? That's the beauty of buying in bulk.

Purchasing ingredients in larger quantities often comes with a lower price per unit, meaning you get more bang for your buck. It's like snagging that coveted two-for-one deal—except it's available all year round, not just during the holiday season.

But before filling up your cart with jumbo-sized bags of rice and multi-packs of chicken, pause for a moment. Consider your storage space and the shelf life of the ingredients. Dry goods like rice and oats have a longer shelf life and are easily stored.

Yet, quickly spoiling items, such as fresh meat or vegetables, should be consumed promptly or frozen to avoid going bad.

Choosing Seasonal Produce: Nature's Calendar of Freshness

Every season brings a new array of fresh fruits and vegetables. Think crisp apples in the fall, juicy oranges in the winter, vibrant peas in the spring, and sun-kissed tomatoes in the summer. These seasonal delights not only add a burst of flavor and color to your dog's meals but can also help you save on your grocery bill.

Seasonal produce tends to be cheaper because it's plentiful and doesn't require long-distance shipping. This situation creates a beneficial scenario where you obtain fresh, tasty produce at a reduced cost and your dog benefits from the nutritional advantages of a diverse diet.

To make the most of seasonal produce, keep an eye on your local grocery store's offerings, visit a nearby farmers market, or even consider growing your fruits and vegetables.

Balancing Cost with Quality: The Value of Wise Choices

We've all heard the saying, "You get what you pay for." It's a reminder that quality often comes at a cost. But when it comes to feeding your dog, quality shouldn't be a luxury—it's a necessity.

Choosing high-quality ingredients means providing your dog with nutrient-dense foods that support their overall health. And while these ingredients may come with a higher price tag, they often offer greater value in the long run.

Take, for instance, a lean cut of meat versus a fattier, cheaper cut. While the latter might save you a few cents now, the lean cut provides more protein and fewer unhealthy fats, contributing to your dog's long-term health.

Similarly, choosing whole grains over refined grains or fresh vegetables over canned ones might cost more, but they pack more nutritional punch.

So, as you navigate the aisles of your grocery store or scroll through your online shopping app, remember to balance cost with quality. Aim to provide your dog the best you can afford because their health is worth every penny.

Ultimately, making economically smart choices regarding homemade dog food is all about planning, smart shopping, and prioritizing quality. With these strategies, you can provide your dog with delicious, nutritious meals without breaking the bank. After all, homemade dog food isn't just about feeding—it's about nourishing. With a bit of thoughtfulness, this nourishment can be achieved in a way that respects your time, budget, and, most importantly, your dog's health.

Finding High-Quality Ingredients: The Treasure Hunt

Identifying Reliable Local Suppliers: The Neighborhood Gems

Think of your local area as a treasure map with potential gold mines of quality ingredients. But how do you discover these hidden gems, you ask? Get ready to don your explorer hat because it's time to embark on a local quest.

First, pay a visit to your local butcher. You'd be surprised at the variety and quality of meats they offer. Not only do they provide an array of lean cuts perfect for your dog's meals, but they can also provide valuable advice on the best choices for your furry friend. Plus, by building a relationship with your local butcher, you can often get tips on when certain items go on sale, helping you score some high-quality bargains.

Next, explore any nearby farms. Many farms sell directly to consumers, offering fresh, organic produce at competitive prices. Some even provide "ugly" fruits and vegetables—those that aren't pretty enough for the supermarket shelves but are just as nutritious —at discounted prices.

Finally, pay attention to pet food stores. Many now stock human-grade meats and vegetables specifically for pet owners who prefer home cooking over commercial pet food. These stores can be a convenient one-stop shop for all your dog's dietary needs.

Shopping at Farmers Markets: The Bounty of the Season

If you've ever strolled through a farmers market, you know it's a sensory delight. The vibrant assortment of fruits and vegetables, the enticing scent of fresh herbs, and the lively activity of shoppers transform it into an experience that surpasses a mere trip to the grocery store.

Farmers markets are superb places to find high-quality, seasonal produce, often at competitive prices. From crisp apples and sweet potatoes in the fall to vibrant peas and juicy tomatoes in the summer, you can find a variety of fruits and vegetables to add to your dog's meals.

But the benefits of shopping at farmer's markets go beyond the fresh produce. You also get to meet the people who grow your food. They can tell you about their farming practices, offer tips on choosing the best produce, and suggest ways to prepare it. Plus, by shopping at farmer's markets, you support local farmers and contribute to your community. It's a win-win situation.

Ordering from Online Retailers: The Digital Marketplace

In this digital age, where you can order everything from books to furniture with a few clicks, why not order your dog's food ingredients online? Numerous online stores provide various items, including meats, grains, fruits, and vegetables, all available for delivery right to your door.

When shopping online, look for retailers who prioritize quality. Read reviews, check ratings, and do your research. Some online shops specialize in organic produce, some offer human-grade meats, and others focus on exotic ingredients that are hard to find in your local stores.

One of the most significant advantages of online shopping is its convenience. You can browse, compare, and order products from the comfort of your home. You can often set up recurring deliveries, ensuring you always have your dog's favorite ingredients.

Remember, while online shopping offers convenience and variety, ensuring you choose high-quality products is still essential. Make sure you do not consider low prices as your only guide; always consider the ingredients' quality and origin.

In the quest for high-quality ingredients for your homemade dog food, remember that it's not about finding the most expensive products or shopping at high-end stores. It's about knowing where to look, asking the right questions, and prioritizing your dog's nutritional needs. By identifying reliable local suppliers, exploring farmer's markets, and navigating online retailers, you can source quality ingredients that contribute to nutritious, delicious meals your dog will love.

Keeping Variety in Your Dog's Diet: The Spice of Life

Think of eating the same meal for breakfast, lunch, and dinner. Day after day. Week after week. Eating like this sounds drab. Now, consider your furry friend. Just like us, they, too, appreciate a little variety in their meals. But ensuring variety in your dog's diet is not just about keeping their taste buds entertained. It's about providing a wide range of nutrients to support their overall health. So, let's explore how you can inject some variety into your dog's homemade meals without causing any digestive upsets.

Introducing New Ingredients Gradually: Easy Does It

Let's say you've decided to introduce a new protein source into your dog's diet, like lamb or fish. Or you've found a new recipe that calls for turnips and are eager to try it out. That's great! But before you rush to serve a bowl full of the new ingredient, remember the golden rule—gradual introduction.

Start by adding a small amount of the new ingredient to your dog's usual meal. Think of it as a culinary sneak peek—a little teaser of what's to come. Watch your dog for signs of digestive or allergic reactions. If they handle the new ingredient well, gradually increase it over several days or weeks. This slow and steady approach helps to familiarize your dog's digestive system with the new ingredient, reducing the risk of upset tummies.

Rotating Protein Sources: The Protein Parade

Protein plays a pivotal role in your dog's diet. It's the building block of muscles, skin, and hair, supports immune function, and provides energy. While chicken might be your go-to protein source, consider branching out to other lean meats like turkey, beef, or lamb. You could also explore fish like salmon or white fish.

Each protein source offers a unique nutrient profile. For instance, salmon contains omega-3 fatty acids, which support skin and coat health, while beef provides good iron and B vitamins. By rotating protein sources, you ensure your dog benefits from the various nutrients each type of protein offers.

However, keep our fundamental principle in mind—introduce any new source of protein slowly. Moreover, always thoroughly cook the meal to eliminate potentially dangerous bacteria.

Experimenting with Different Types of Vegetables: The Veggie Variety Show

Vegetables are a fortified, rich source of vitamins and minerals. They also provide fiber, which supports healthy digestion. But suppose your dog's vegetable intake is limited to peas and carrots. In that case, they need to include the nutritional diversity vegetables provide.

Consider introducing a range of colorful veggies to your dog's diet. Red bell peppers, spinach, sweet potatoes, zucchini—the options are plentiful. Each vegetable offers a unique mix of nutrients. Spinach is an excellent provider of vitamins A, C, and K. Sweet potatoes are rich in fiber and beta-carotene.

Again, introduce new veggies gradually and cooked to make them easier for your dog to digest. And remember, not all vegetables are safe for dogs—avoid onions, garlic, and avocados.

So there we have it—a roadmap to adding variety to your dog's homemade meals. By introducing new ingredients gradually, rotating protein sources, and experimenting with different vegetables, you can transform mealtime into a culinary adventure for your furry friend. And more importantly, you can provide a balanced, nutrient-rich diet that supports their overall health.

With that, we've explored a lot of the basics of homemade dog food. We've journeyed from understanding the fundamentals of canine nutrition to the practical aspects of cooking, portioning, and storing meals. We've tackled challenges like time constraints and budgeting and celebrated the joy of serving nutritious, homemade meals that get our dogs' tails wagging.

But our journey doesn't end here. We have one more chapter. In our final chapter, we will explore monitoring health changes after transitioning your dog to homemade dog food. So, keep those aprons ready, those pots simmering, and those tails wagging. The adventure continues!

Doberman Pinschers are the sleek, stylish supermodels of the dog world, with a gaze as sharp as their intellect. They're like four-legged secret agents, always on high alert and ready to protect their loved ones with a mix of grace and power. Yet, they're just as happy to curl up by your feet, proving that even the fiercest warriors need a cuddle.

12

PAW-SITIVE CHANGES: YOUR DOG'S HEALTH TRANSFORMATION

V isualize the look of delight on your child's face when they unwrap a surprise gift. Now, imagine that joy mirrored in your dog's eyes as they discover the wealth of flavors and textures in their new homemade diet. But the magic of homemade dog food isn't just in the happy tail wag or the eager anticipation at mealtime. It's in the subtle yet profound changes in your dog's health that follow.

In this chapter, we'll learn how to be vigilant observers, noticing the transformation in our dogs as they embrace their new diet. With our love for our furry companions guiding us, we'll understand how to spot signs of improved health and vitality.

Monitoring Health Changes after Switching to Homemade Food

When you start feeding your dog a homemade diet, it's like giving their health a fresh coat of paint. The changes may not be noticeable overnight, but each stroke adds to the vibrant picture of health with time. Here's what to look out for:

Observing Changes in Energy Levels: The Zoomies Indicator

Remember those lazy afternoons when your dog would rather nap than fetch the ball? Well, prepare for a change. One of the first improvements you might notice when you switch to homemade dog food is an increase in your dog's energy levels.

Just like us, dogs thrive on a balanced, nutrient-rich diet. When their bodies receive the right fuel, they will likely have more energy for walks, playtime, and even the beloved Zoomies. And as their energy levels improve, so does their overall quality of life.

The next time your dog insists on an extra round of fetch, take a moment to celebrate. It's a sign your pup's body is responding well to a new diet.

Noticing Improvements in Coat Condition: The Glossy Coat Club

Rushing your fingers through your dog's soft, shiny coat is a particular joy. It's a sensory reminder of your dog's health and well-being. And with a homemade diet, this joy may be magnified.

A balanced homemade diet can do wonders for your dog's skin and coat. The right blend of proteins, fatty acids, and vitamins can help maintain healthy skin and promote a glossy coat.

When you notice your dog's coat becoming shinier and softer or when their dry skin starts showing signs of improvement, take it as a thumbs up from their body. It's their way of saying, "I'm loving this new diet!"

Tracking Weight Changes: The Wagging Scale

Weight is a crucial indicator of a dog's health. It's a balancing act—too thin, and they may not get enough nutrients; too heavy, and they risk developing various health issues. When you switch your dog to a homemade diet, one of the significant changes may be in their weight.

But remember, weight loss or gain should be gradual. Rapid changes could signal that something's off balance. Regular weigh-ins can help you monitor changes and adjust portion sizes or ingredients.

So, when your dog achieves and maintains their ideal weight, it's a victory worth celebrating. It's a testament to the power of a balanced, homemade diet and your commitment to their health.

Embracing homemade dog food is like embarking on a health makeover for your dog. And as with any makeover, the results are rewarding. From improved energy levels and a shinier coat to a healthier weight, these positive changes are a testament to your dog's body loving the new diet.

As you celebrate these victories, big and small, you'll find that the effort of preparing homemade meals is worth every bit. After all, each meal is a building block, contributing to a happier, healthier life for your furry friend. So, here's to the joy of homemade dog food—a pleasure savored one meal at a time, one health victory at a time.

The Role of Regular Vet Checkups: Your Ally in Canine Health

Scheduling Routine Vet Visits: Marking the Canine Calendar

Think of your dog's vet as a co-pilot who understands your dog's health journey and can guide you through the turbulence. Regular checkups are like touchpoints, opportunities for your vet to assess your dog's well-being and for you to voice any concerns.

But how often should these touchpoints occur? For most dogs, an annual checkup is sufficient. However, puppies, elderly dogs, or dogs with chronic health conditions could benefit from more frequent visits. Your vet can recommend a schedule based on your dog's specific needs.

During these checkups, your vet will assess your dog's weight, heart rate, temperature, and overall condition. If needed, they may also perform blood, urine, or other diagnostic tests. A thorough health assessment can help detect possible issues before they become larger problems.

Discussing Diet Changes with Your Vet: The Nutritional Dialogue

As you transition your furry pet to a homemade diet, your vet becomes an even more critical ally. They can provide guidance on nutritional requirements, help you adjust recipes or portion sizes, and monitor your dog's response to the new diet.

When you discuss diet changes with your vet, be open and specific. Share the recipes you're using, the ingredients you're including, and how much you feed your dog. If you're using supplements, mention those too. The more information your vet has, the better they can guide you.

Remember, your vet isn't there to judge but to support you. They share your goal of ensuring your dog is healthy and happy. So, don't hesitate to ask questions, seek advice, or voice concerns.

Interpreting Lab Results: The Canine Health Report Card

Lab results are a confusing jumble of numbers and jargon. But to your vet, they're a treasure trove of information about your dog's health.

For instance, a complete blood count (CBC) can provide information about your dog's red and white blood cells and platelets. It can indicate conditions like anemia, infections, or clotting problems. A blood chemistry panel, on the other hand, can give insights into your dog's liver and kidney function, electrolyte status, and more.

Your vet can interpret these results and explain their meaning in a language you understand. They can identify abnormalities, explain potential causes, and suggest next steps.

Lab results also provide a baseline to monitor changes over time. Results can be beneficial as you transition your dog to a homemade diet. By comparing lab results before and after the diet change, your vet can assess how well your dog responds to their new diet.

While homemade dog food has many benefits, it does not replace regular vet care. Your vet is essential to your dog's health journey, providing valuable insights, advice, and support. Regular checkups, open communication, and understanding lab results are all part of maintaining your dog's health. So, value this partnership, and remember that you and your vet are on the same team—the team that wants the best for your beloved canine companion.

Remember, anyone can cook a meal. But cooking a meal that nourishes, delights, and supports the health of your dog—that's something special. It's a labor of love, a commitment to your dog's well-being, and a journey worth every step. So, keep those pots simmering, those tails wagging, and those hearts overflowing with love. Here's to the joy of homemade dog food, one paw-licking meal at a time.

Celebrating Success Stories of Health Improvement

Sharing Your Own Success Story: The Power of Personal Experience

Imagine you're at a dog park, watching your pooch frolic with newfound friends. A fellow pet parent, intrigued by your dog's energy and shiny coat, starts a conversation. It is your moment to shine, your stage to share your homemade dog food success story.

Tell them about how you swapped kibble for fresh, wholesome meals. Please talk about the changes you've noticed, whether it's your dog's increased energy, improved skin and coat, or stable weight. Share your challenges, victories, and the lessons you've learned along the way.

Your story, told from the heart, could inspire others to embark on their homemade dog food adventure. It could spark curiosity, answer questions, and even address doubts or misconceptions. And it could serve as a testament to the transformative power of a homemade diet.

Learning from Other Dog Owners' Experiences: A Community of Knowledge

The world of homemade dog food is vibrant, diverse, and insightful. Other pet parents, each with unique stories, form a community of knowledge invaluable for anyone new to this path.

Seek out these stories. Listen to the pet parent at the dog park, the neighbor who swears by meals, or the friend who's always sharing dog food recipes. Join online forums, follow relevant blogs, and engage with social media groups centered around homemade dog food.

Each story you encounter is a nugget of wisdom, a slice of experience that adds to your understanding. You'll discover new ingredients to try, pick up time-saving tips, and learn about potential pitfalls to avoid. You'll find inspiration in their successes and learn from their mistakes. And you'll realize that you're part of a larger community committed to providing the best for their furry friends.

Encouraging Others to Try Homemade Dog Food: Spreading the Word

As you navigate your homemade dog food path, remember to extend a helping hand to those a few steps behind. Share your experiences, your recipes, and your tips. Answer questions, address concerns, and offer reassurances.

Encourage your friends, neighbors, or fellow pet parents to try homemade dog food at the dog park. Offer to help them get started, whether by sharing a simple recipe or assisting them in calculating portion sizes.

Each conversation you have, each tip you share, and each question you answer could make a difference. It could be the nudge someone needs to try homemade dog food. And it could contribute to more dogs enjoying the benefits of a balanced, nutritious, homemade diet.

In the grand scheme, your success with homemade dog food is more than just about your dog. It's about sharing your knowledge, learning from others, and encouraging more pet parents to try this rewarding path. It's about celebrating the positive impact of homemade meals on dogs' health and spreading the word about its benefits. Keep sharing, keep learning, and keep encouraging. The world of homemade dog food is more prosperous and vibrant with you.

A Never-Ending Quest: Achieving Peak Canine Health

Committing to Continuous Learning: A Pledge to Your Pooch

Imagine walking down a road that never ends. Intriguing. This is similar to the path of continuous learning you embark on when you commit to homemade dog food. This journey is rich with new knowledge, perspectives, and experiences that broaden your understanding and skills.

You're learning with each meal you prepare, each recipe you try, and each health improvement you notice in your dog. You're discovering which ingredients your dog loves, which offer the most nutritional benefits, and how varied portions affect your dog's health. And with this learning, you're becoming a more confident and competent cook for your canine.

Adjusting Your Approach as Needed: The Flexibility Factor

Just as a river changes its course based on the landscape, you, too, might need to adjust your approach based on your dog's evolving needs. This flexibility is crucial in ensuring your homemade meals nourish your dog and support their health.

For example, noticing your once energetic dog becoming lethargic might indicate that they're not getting enough calories. You could then adjust their meals by adding more protein or healthy fats. Alternatively, suppose your dog starts to gain unwanted weight. In that case, you should reduce portions or include more low-calorie vegetables in their meals.

The goal is to keep your dog healthy and joyful; sometimes, achieving this goal requires adjustments. Embrace these changes as part of the process, and remember, each adjustment brings you one step closer to providing the best nutrition for your dog.

Celebrating Small Victories: The Joy of Little Triumphs

Every time your dog gobbles up a homemade meal, it's a small victory. Every wag of their tail, every sparkle in their eye, and every bound of energy is a celebration of the positive impact of homemade food on their health.

These victories may seem small, but they're significant. They prove that your efforts are paying off and that the time and energy you're investing in preparing homemade meals enhance your dog's health and happiness.

So, don't wait for a monumental moment to pat yourself on the back. Celebrate each small victory, each positive change, and each successful meal. These are the moments that make the journey worthwhile.

As you navigate the path of homemade dog food, remember it's a continuous journey of learning, adjusting, and celebrating. It's a commitment to your dog's health and a testament to your love for them. So, keep exploring, keep learning, and keep celebrating. Your dog's health transformation is an ongoing journey that's as rewarding as the destination itself.

Boxers are the comedians of the canine world, with a bounce in their step and a wiggle in their walk that can't help but make you smile. They're like exuberant, slobbery kids in fur coats, always up for a game or a goof, yet they guard their families with hearts as big as their grins. Just try keeping a straight face when a Boxer is around; it's like trying to resist a wagging tail – impossible!

A FINAL INVITATION

Thank you for joining me in **Easy and Healthy Homemade Dog Food Recipes and Guide.** Your commitment to your dog's nutrition is inspiring. I'm grateful to share my knowledge and recipes. If this book improves your dog's health or mealtime, please consider leaving a review on **Amazon.** Your feedback helps guide others and contributes to a community dedicated to healthy pet care. Share your experiences and insights to support our mission of better canine nutrition and wellness. Your input is invaluable, and I look forward to your reflections.

Scan the QR Code to Leave Your Review

FREE COLOR IMAGES AND FREE TRANSITION GUIDE

To Access FREE Full-Color Images of Recipes and Your FREE 31-Day Transition Guide, Scan the QR Code Below

CONCLUSION

Well, my fellow dog-loving comrades, we've ended our tail-wagging adventure. But let's be honest: is there ever an end to the wonderful world of homemade dog food? I want to think of it more as a pause, a moment to take a breather and look back at the trail we've blazed together.

So, let's take a moment to celebrate the joyful journey of homemade dog food. You've swapped out store-bought kibble for fresh, wholesome meals, learned to calculate portion sizes, and even got the hang of meal prepping. Bravo, my friend! You've come a long way from the hesitant newbie wondering if they could pull off this homemade dog food.

And the result of your efforts? Healthier, happier dogs. That's right. Each wag of the tail, each excited dance at mealtime, and each shiny coat is a testament to the positive impact of your labor of love. It's like we've unlocked a secret level in the game of canine health, and oh, what a rewarding level it is!

Let's remember that this journey wasn't all sunshine and rainbows. There were challenges, doubts, and maybe even a few kitchen disasters. (If you've never accidentally turned the kitchen into a scene from a food fight... are you even trying?) But that's all part of the learning and growing process. And you've handled it with the grace of a dog trying to catch their tail—stumbling, twirling, but ultimately having a blast.

So, what's next? Well, my friend, I have a small request. You see, just like how a good belly rub gets our dogs' legs kicking with joy, spreading the love for homemade dog food gives me a similar kick.

I encourage you to share your homemade dog food journey— the ups, the downs, the drool-worthy successes. Tell your friends about it, chat with fellow dog walkers in the park, or share your dog's meal-time snaps on social media (extra points for adorable messy-face pictures).

Let's create a community of homemade dog food champions, one dog parent at a time. Because every dog deserves a diet that's as fresh, wholesome, and loving as they are, and together, we can make that happen.

So, here's to you, my fellow explorer of homemade dog food territory. Your journey may have started with a simple curiosity, a desire to do the best for your furry pal. But look at you now, a full-fledged homemade dog food aficionado, making a real difference in your dog's health and happiness.

Remember, the journey doesn't end here. Keep exploring, learning, and, most importantly, loving your canine companion through the fabulous food you make. Because, in the end, that's what matters most—the love we share with our dogs, one delicious, nutritious meal at a time.

Irish Setters are the flame-haired enchanters of the dog world, with a zest for life as infectious as their boundless energy. They're like four-legged fireworks, lighting up every room enthusiastically and elegantly. With a setter around, life is never dull — it's an endless game of chase, where every leaf and butterfly is a potential friend or foe, all pursued with the grace of a dancer and the speed of a sprinter.

A WORD FROM THE AUTHOR

As we reach the end of *Easy and Healthy Homemade Dog Food Recipes and Guide*, I want to extend my heartfelt gratitude to you, my readers. Your support and dedication to providing the best for your furry friends have driven this journey. I hope this book has inspired you, offered new insights, and brought you closer to understanding the nutritional needs of your beloved pets. Your commitment to their well-being is a testament to the incredible bond we share with our dogs, and it has been an honor to be a part of your journey towards healthier, happier companions.

Looking ahead, I am optimistic about the future we can create for our pets. With each recipe you try and each new habit you form, you contribute to a more robust, vibrant life for your dogs. Remember, the journey to optimal health is ongoing, and every small step you take makes a difference. I encourage you to keep exploring, learning, and growing in your knowledge of canine nutrition. The road ahead is exciting, and the possibilities are endless when it comes to enhancing the lives of our four-legged family members.

I wish you and your pets all the best as you continue this rewarding path. May your kitchens be filled with the joy of cooking, your homes with the joyful barking of your dogs, and your hearts with the love they unconditionally give us. Thank you for allowing me to be a part of your adventure. Here's to many more years of health, happiness, and tail-wagging meals. Cheers to a bright future together, nourishing the bodies and spirits of our beloved dogs.

ALSO FROM PAGETURNER PUBLISHERS

Unlock health and wellness with this guide to all-natural herbal teas. Discover the science, history, and benefits of herbal tea, including:

- **Key benefits** and the science of health improvement
- Criteria for **quality herbs and** ingredients
- **5 enriching tea-drinking rituals**
- **100 fresh and delicious recipes**

Gain insights into selecting high-quality, organic herbs and teas on a budget. A holistic approach to rejuvenate your senses and enhance overall well-being through the power of herbal tea.

Scan the QR Code to Purchase Now!

Explore the power of **conscious breathing** with **21 techniques** to de-stress, re-energize, and manage pain. This guide covers:

- **Deep, Box, and Alternate Nostril Breathing**
- **Step-by-step instructions** and **integration tips**
- **Focus** and **energy** exercises
- **Stress management** strategies

A transformative tool for immediate well-being benefits.

Scan the QR Code to Purchase Now!

REFERENCES

Dog Nutrition: Essential Nutrients for Health and Feeding ... https://www.webmd.com/pets/dogs/dog-nutrition

Dog Life Stages Nutrition Guide https://natureslogic.com/bog/dog-life-stages-nutrition-guide/

common food allergen sources in dogs and cats - PMC https://www.ncbi.nlm.nih.gov/pmc/articles/PMC4710035/

Hydration Is Important to Your Dog's Health https://www.diamondpet.com/blog/health/renal/hydration-important-dogs-health/

Feeding Growing Puppies - VCA Animal Hospitals https://vcahospitals.com/know-your-pet/feeding-growing-puppies

Vet-Approved Homemade Dog Food Recipes https://www.thesprucepets.com/homemade-dog-food-recipes-5200240

Feeding Mature and Senior Dogs - VCA Animal Hospitals https://vcahospitals.com/know-your-pet/feeding-mature-and-senior-dogs

Nutritional Needs for Pregnant Dogs & Nursing Dogs https://www.iams.com/dog/dog-articles/nutritional-needs-pregnant-and-nursing-dogs

Food Allergies in Dogs - VCA Animal Hospitals https://vcahospitals.com/know-your-pet/food-allergies-in-dogs

What's the Best Food for Dogs With Sensitive Stomachs? https://www.petmd.com/dog/nutrition/whats-best-food-dogs-sensitive-stomachs

Nutrition - HeartSmart – Information on Pets with Heart Disease https://heartsmart.vet.tufts.edu/nutrition/

How to Help Your Dog Lose Weight https://www.akc.org/expert-advice/nutrition/dog-obesity-safe-weight-loss/

How to Transition you Dog onto a Fresh Food Diet https://thecaninehealthnut.com/transitiondogtonewfood/

Introduction to Digestive Disorders of Dogs - Dog Owners https://www.merckvetmanual.com/dog-owners/digestive-disorders-of-dogs/introduction-to-digestive-disorders-of-dogs

11 Tips for Feeding a Picky Dog https://www.stellaandchewys.com/dogs/picky-eater/

When to Consult a Vet: Navigating Diet Shifts for Dogs - Diarrice https://diarrice.com/when-to-consult-a-vet-navigating-diet-shifts-for-dogs/

YOUR DOG'S NUTRITIONAL NEEDS https://nap.nationalacademies.org/resource/10668/dog_nutrition_final_fix.pdf

Unleashing the Benefits of Homemade Fresh Dog Food https://www.akc.org/expert-advice/nutrition/benefits-of-homemade-dog-food/

common food allergen sources in dogs and cats - PMC https://www.ncbi.nlm.nih.gov/pmc/articles/PMC4710035/

NEW Gently Cooked Recipes for Dogs & Cats https://primalpetfoods.com/blogs/news/new-gently-cooked-recipes-for-dogs-cats

5 Cheap Homemade Dog Food Recipes https://topdogtips.com/cheap-homemade-dog-food-recipes/

Life Stage Nutrition for Pets https://www.texvetpets.org/article/life-stage-nutrition-for-pets/

Grains Or No Grains: Addressing Pet Owner Concerns https://vetmed.tamu.edu/news/pet-talk/grains-or-no-grains-addressing-pet-owner-concerns/

Food Allergies in Dogs - VCA Animal Hospitals https://vcahospitals.com/know-your-pet/food-allergies-in-dogs

FDA Grain-Free Diet Alert: What Dog Owners Need to Know https://www.akc.org/expert-advice/nutrition/fda-grain-free-diet-alert-dcm/

Healthy Meat for Dogs: Beef, Chicken, Duck, Turkey, Lamb ... https://www.thehonestkitchen.com/blogs/pet-food-ingredients/healthy-meat-for-dogs

Benefits of vegetables for dogs - Guides https://www.bigdogpetfoods.com/guides/benefits-of-vegetables-for-dogs

common food allergen sources in dogs and cats - PMC https://www.ncbi.nlm.nih.gov/pmc/articles/PMC4710035/

The Benefits of Homemade Dog Treats https://www.amli.com/blog/the-benefits-of-homemade-dog-treats

Can Dogs Eat Peanut Butter? https://www.akc.org/expert-advice/nutrition/can-dogs-eat-peanut-butter/

Easy DIY Dog Chews from Dehydrated Sweet Potatoes https://www.thepurposefulpantry.com/easy-diy-dog-chews/

Pumpkin for Dogs: Everything You Need to Know https://www.justfoodfordogs.com/lifestyle/pumpkin-for-dogs-everything-you-need-to-know.html

How To Store Homemade Dog Food: 6 Vet-Approved Tips https://www.hepper.com/how-to-store-homemade-dog-food/

Dog Meal Prep: How to Prepare Dog Food in Bulk https://www.akc.org/expert-advice/nutrition/dog-meal-prep-dog-food-in-bulk/

How To Store Homemade Dog Food: 6 Vet-Approved Tips https://www.hepper.com/how-to-store-homemade-dog-food/

The 7 Best Dog Food Storage Containers, Tested ... https://www.thesprucepets.com/best-dog-food-storage-containers-4797025

How Many Calories Does a Dog Need? https://www.petmd.com/dog/nutrition/how-many-calories-does-a-dog-need

Nutritional Needs of Different Breeds of Dogs https://www.webmd.com/pets/dogs/features/food-breed

The Effects of Overfeeding and Underfeeding in dogs https://colaskitchen.com/blog-posts/dog-diet-overfeeding-underfeeding-effects

The Top 7 Most Common Food Allergens For Dogs https://www.rover.com/blog/7-common-food-allergens-dogs/

Homemade Dog Food Recipes: Choosing Balanced ... https://www.akc.org/expert-advice/nutrition/choosing-ingredients-homemade-dog-food/

Affordable Homemade Dog Food Recipes and Tips https://thedollarstretcher.com/family-finances/affordable-homemade-dog-food-recipes-and-tips/

Essential Dog Food Ingredients for Healthy Dogs https://www.akc.org/expert-advice/nutrition/essential-dog-food-ingredients-for-healthy-dogs/

Homemade Dog Food Recipes: Choosing Balanced ... https://www.akc.org/expert-advice/nutrition/choosing-ingredients-homemade-dog-food/

Homemade Dog Food: Is It Healthy to Cook for Your Dog https://www.petmd.com/dog/nutrition/how-make-sure-your-homemade-dog-food-delivers-right-nutrients

Homemade dog food recipes can be risky business, study ... https://www.ucdavis.edu/news/homemade-dog-food-recipes-can-be-risky-business-study-finds

Pet owners share their homemade diet success stories https://www.washingtonpost.com/local/pet-owners-share-their-homemade-diet-success-stories/2014/11/06/1bc0d4a8-5fa7-11e4-8b9e-2ccdac31a031_story.html

Homemade Dog Food: Vet-Approved Recipes For Dogs https://www.thewildest.com/dog-nutrition/vet-approved-homemade-dog-food

All images were generated with the assistance of DALL-E.